Production-Ready Microservices

Building Standardized Systems Across
an Engineering Organization

Susan J. Fowler

Beijing · Boston · Farnham · Sebastopol · Tokyo

Production-Ready Microservices

by Susan J. Fowler

Printed in the United States of America.

Published by O'Reilly Media, Inc., 1005 Gravenstein Highway North, Sebastopol, CA 95472.

O'Reilly books may be purchased for educational, business, or sales promotional use. Online editions are also available for most titles (*http://oreilly.com/safari*). For more information, contact our corporate/institutional sales department: 800-998-9938 or *corporate@oreilly.com*.

Editors: Nan Barber and Brian Foster
Production Editor: Kristen Brown
Copyeditor: Amanda Kersey
Proofreader: Jasmine Kwityn

Indexer: Wendy Catalano
Interior Designer: David Futato
Cover Designer: Karen Montgomery
Illustrator: Rebecca Demarest

December 2016:   First Edition

Revision History for the First Edition
2016-11-23:   First Release

See *http://oreilly.com/catalog/errata.csp?isbn=9781491965979* for release details.

978-1-491-96597-9

[LSI]

Table of Contents

Preface... vii

1. Microservices... 1
   From Monoliths to Microservices   2
   Microservice Architecture   9
   The Microservice Ecosystem   11
     Layer 1: Hardware   12
     Layer 2: Communication   14
     Layer 3: The Application Platform   16
     Layer 4: Microservices   19
   Organizational Challenges   20
     The Inverse Conway's Law   21
     Technical Sprawl   22
     More Ways to Fail   23
     Competition for Resources   24

2. Production-Readiness.. 25
   The Challenges of Microservice Standardization   25
   Availability: The Goal of Standardization   26
   Production-Readiness Standards   28
     Stability   29
     Reliability   29
     Scalability   30
     Fault Tolerance and Catastrophe-Preparedness   32
     Performance   33
     Monitoring   34
     Documentation   35
   Implementing Production-Readiness   37

3. Stability and Reliability. 41

Principles of Building Stable and Reliable Microservices   41

The Development Cycle   42

The Deployment Pipeline   44

    Staging   45

    Canary   50

    Production   51

    Enforcing Stable and Reliable Deployment   52

Dependencies   53

Routing and Discovery   55

Deprecation and Decommissioning   56

Evaluate Your Microservice   57

    The Development Cycle   57

    The Deployment Pipeline   57

    Dependencies   57

    Routing and Discovery   58

    Deprecation and Decommissioning   58

4. Scalability and Performance. 59

Principles of Microservice Scalability and Performance   59

Knowing the Growth Scale   60

    The Qualitative Growth Scale   61

    The Quantitative Growth Scale   62

Efficient Use of Resources   63

Resource Awareness   64

    Resource Requirements   64

    Resource Bottlenecks   65

Capacity Planning   65

Dependency Scaling   67

Traffic Management   68

Task Handling and Processing   69

    Programming Language Limitations   69

    Handling Requests and Processing Tasks Efficiently   70

Scalable Data Storage   71

    Database Choice in Microservice Ecosystems   72

    Database Challenges in Microservice Architecture   73

Evaluate Your Microservice   73

    Knowing the Growth Scale   74

    Efficient Use of Resources   74

    Resource Awareness   74

    Capacity Planning   74

    Dependency Scaling   74

Traffic Management	75
Task Handling and Processing	75
Scalable Data Storage	75

5. Fault Tolerance and Catastrophe-Preparedness.................................. **77**
Principles of Building Fault-Tolerant Microservices	77
Avoiding Single Points of Failure	79
Catastrophes and Failure Scenarios	80
Common Failures Across an Ecosystem	81
Hardware Failures	83
Communication-Level and Application Platform–Level Failures	84
Dependency Failures	86
Internal (Microservice) Failures	88
Resiliency Testing	89
Code Testing	90
Load Testing	91
Chaos Testing	94
Failure Detection and Remediation	96
Incidents and Outages	97
Appropriate Categorization	98
The Five Stages of Incident Response	99
Evaluate Your Microservice	102
Avoiding Single Points of Failure	102
Catastrophes and Failure Scenarios	102
Resiliency Testing	103
Failure Detection and Remediation	103

6. Monitoring... **105**
Principles of Microservice Monitoring	105
Key Metrics	106
Logging	109
Dashboards	110
Alerting	112
Setting up Effective Alerting	112
Handling Alerts	113
On-Call Rotations	114
Evaluate Your Microservice	115
Key Metrics	115
Logging	115
Dashboards	116
Alerting	116
On-Call Rotations	116

7. Documentation and Understanding. 117
    Principles of Microservice Documentation and Understanding   117
    Microservice Documentation   119
      Description   120
      Architecture Diagram   121
      Contact and On-Call Information   122
      Links   122
      Onboarding and Development Guide   122
      Request Flows, Endpoints, and Dependencies   123
      On-Call Runbooks   123
      FAQ   124
    Microservice Understanding   125
      Architecture Reviews   126
      Production-Readiness Audits   127
      Production-Readiness Roadmaps   128
      Production-Readiness Automation   128
    Evaluate Your Microservice   129
      Microservice Documentation   130
      Microservice Understanding   130

A. Production-Readiness Checklist. 131

B. Evaluate Your Microservice. 135

Glossary. 143

Index. 149

Preface

This book was born out of a production-readiness initiative I began running several months after I joined Uber Technologies as a site reliability engineer (SRE). Uber's gigantic, monolithic API was slowly being broken into microservices, and at the time I joined, there were over a thousand microservices that had been split from the API and were running alongside it. Each of these microservices was designed, built, and maintained by an owning development team, and over 85% of these services had little to no SRE involvement, nor any access to SRE resources.

Hiring SREs and building SRE teams is an absurdly difficult task, because SREs are probably the hardest type of engineers to find: site reliability engineering as a field is still relatively new, and SREs must be experts (at least to some degree) in software engineering, systems engineering, and distributed systems architecture. There was no way to quickly staff all of the teams with their own embedded SRE team, and so my team (the Consulting SRE Team) was born. Our directive from above was simple: find a way to drive high standards across the 85% of microservices that had no SRE involvement.

Our mission was simple, and the directive was vague enough that it allowed me and my team a considerable amount of freedom to define a set of standards that every microservice at Uber could follow. Coming up with high standards that could apply to every single microservice running within this large engineering organization was not easy, and so, with some help from my amazing colleague Rick Boone (whose high standards for the microservices he supported inspired this book), I created a detailed checklist of the standards that I believed every service at Uber should meet before being allowed to host production traffic.

Doing so required identifying a set of overall, umbrella principles that every specific requirement would fall under, and we came up with eight such principles: every microservice at Uber, we said, should be *stable, reliable, scalable, fault tolerant, performant, monitored, documented*, and *prepared for any catastrophe*. Under each of these principles were separate criteria that defined what it meant for a service to be stable, reliable, scalable, fault tolerant, performant, monitored, documented, and prepared for any catastrophe. Importantly, we demanded that each principle be quantifiable, and that each criterion provide us with measurable results that dramatically increased the availability of our microservices. A service that met these criteria, a service that fit these requirements, we deemed *production-ready*.

Driving these standards across teams in an effective and efficient way was the next step. I created a careful process in which SRE teams met with business-critical services (services whose outages would bring the application down), ran architecture reviews with the teams, put together audits of their services (simple checklists that said "yes" or "no" to whether the service met each production-readiness requirement), created detailed roadmaps (step-by-step guides that detailed how to bring the service in question to a production-ready state), and assigned production-readiness scores to each service.

Running the architecture reviews was the most important part of the process: my team would gather all of the developers working on a service in a conference room and ask them to whiteboard the architecture of their service in 30 minutes or less. Doing this allowed both my team and the host team to quickly and easily identify where and why the service was failing: when a microservice was diagrammed in all of its glory (endpoints, request flows, dependencies and all), every point of failure stood out like a sore thumb.

Every architecture review produced a great deal of work. After each review, we'd work through the checklist and see if the service met any of the production-readiness requirements, and then we'd share this audit out with the managers and developers of the team. Scoring was added to the audits when I realized that the *production-ready or not* idea was simply not granular enough to be useful when we evaluated the production-readiness of services, so each requirement was assigned a certain number of points and then an overall score given to the service.

From the audits came roadmaps. Roadmaps contained a list of the production-readiness requirements that the service did not meet, along with links to information about recent outages caused by not meeting that requirement, descriptions of the work that needed to be done in order to meet the requirement, a link to an open task, and the name of the developer(s) assigned to the relevant task.

After doing my own production-readiness check on this process (also known as Susan-Fowler's-production-readiness-process-as-a-service), I knew that the next step would need to be the automation of the entire process that would run on all Uber microservices, all of the time. At the time of the writing of this book, this entire production-readiness system is being automated by an amazing SRE team at Uber led by the fearless Roxana del Toro.

Each of the production-readiness requirements within the production-readiness standards and the details of their implementation came out of countless hours of careful, deliberate work by myself and my colleagues in the Uber SRE organization. In making the list of requirements, and in trying to implement them across all Uber microservices, we took countless notes, argued with one another at great length, and researched whatever we could find in the current microservice literature (which is very sparse, and almost nonexistent). I met with a wide variety of microservice developer teams, both at Uber and at other companies, trying to determine how microservices could be standardized and whether there existed a universal set of standardization principles that could be applied to every microservice at every company and produce measurable, business-impactful results. From those notes, arguments, meetings, and research came the foundations of this book.

It wasn't until after I began sharing my work with site reliability engineers and software engineers at other companies in the Bay Area that I realized how novel it was, not only in the SRE world, but in the tech industry as a whole. When engineers started asking me for every bit of information and guidance I could give them on standardizing their microservices and making their microservices production-ready, I began writing.

At the time of writing, there exists very little literature on microservice standardization and very few guides to maintaining and building the microservice ecosystem. Moreover, there are no books that answer the question many engineers have after splitting their monolithic application into microservices: what do we do next? The ambitious goal of this book is to fill that gap, and to answer precisely that question. In a nutshell, this is the book I wish that I had when I began standardizing microservices at Uber.

Who This Book Is Written For

This book is primarily written for software engineers and site reliability engineers who have either split a monolith and are wondering "what's next?", or who are building microservices from the ground up and want to design stable, reliable, scalable, fault-tolerant, performant microservices from the get-go.

However, the relevance of the principles within this book is not limited to the primary audience. Many of the principles, from good monitoring to successfully scaling an application, can be applied to improve services and applications of any size and architecture at any organization. Engineers, engineering managers, product managers, and high-level company executives may find this book useful for a variety of reasons, including determining standards for their application(s), understanding changes in organizational structure that result from architecture decisions, or for determining and driving the architectural and operational vision of their engineering organization(s).

I do assume that the reader is familiar with the basic concepts of microservices, with microservice architecture, and with the fundamentals of modern distributed systems —readers who understand these concepts well will gain the most from this book. For readers unfamiliar with these topics, I've dedicated the first chapter to a short overview of microservice architecture, the microservice ecosystem, organizational challenges that accompany microservices, and the nitty-gritty reality of breaking a monolithic application into microservices.

What This Book Is Not

This book is not a step-by-step how-to guide: it is not an explicit tutorial on how to do each of the things covered in its chapters. Writing such a tutorial would require many, many volumes: each section of each of the chapters within this book could be expanded into its own book.

As a result, this is a highly abstract book, written to be general enough that the lessons learned here can be applied to nearly every microservice at nearly every company, yet specific and granular enough that it can be incorporated into an engineering organization and provide real, tangible guidance on how to improve and standardize microservices. Because the microservice ecosystem will differ from company to company, there isn't any benefit to be found in taking a step-by-step authoritative or educational approach. Instead, I've decided to introduce concepts, explain their importance to building production-ready microservices, offer examples of each concept, and share strategies for their implementation.

Importantly, this book is not an encyclopedic account of all the possible ways that microservices and microservice ecosystems can be built and run. I will be the first to admit that there are many valid ways to build and run microservices and microservice ecosystems. (For example, there are many different ways to test new builds aside from the staging-canary-production approach that I introduce and advocate for in Chapter 3, *Stability and Reliability*). But some ways are better than others, and I have tried as hard as possible to present only the best ways to build and run production-ready microservices and apply each production-readiness principle across engineering organizations.

In addition, technology moves and changes remarkably fast. Whenever and wherever possible, I have tried to avoid limiting the reader to an existing technology or set of technologies to implement. For example, rather than advocating that every microservice use Kafka for logging, I present the important aspects of production-ready logging and leave the choice of specific technology and the actual implementation to the reader.

Finally, this book is not a description of the Uber engineering organization. The principles, standards, examples, and strategies are not specific to Uber nor exclusively inspired by Uber: they have been developed and inspired by microservices of many technology companies and can be applied to any microservice ecosystem. This is not a descriptive or historical account, but a prescriptive guide to building production-ready microservices.

How To Use This Book

There are several ways you can use this book.

The first approach is the least involved one: to read only the chapters you are interested in, and skim through (or skip) the rest. There is much to be gained from this approach: you'll find yourself introduced to new concepts, gain insight on concepts you may be familiar with, and walk away with new ways to think about aspects of software engineering and microservice architecture that you may find useful in your day-to-day life and work.

Another approach is a slightly more involved one, in which you can skim through the book, reading carefully the sections that are relevant to your needs, and then apply some of the principles and standards to your microservice(s). For example, if your microservice(s) is in need of improved monitoring, you could skim through the majority of the book, reading only Chapter 6, *Monitoring*, closely and then use the material in this chapter to improve the monitoring, alerting, and outage response processes of your service(s).

The last approach you could take is (probably) the most rewarding one, and the one you should take if your goal is to fully standardize either the microservice you are responsible for or all of the microservices at your company so that it or they are truly production-ready. If your goal is to make your microservice(s) stable, reliable, scalable, fault tolerant, performant, properly monitored, well documented, and prepared for any catastrophe, you'll want to take this approach. To accomplish this, each chapter should be read carefully, each standard understood, and each requirement adjusted and applied to fit the needs of your microservice(s).

At the end of each of the standardization chapters (Chapters 3-7), you will find a section titled "Evaluate Your Microservice," which contains a short list of questions you can ask about your microservice. The questions are organized by topic so that you (the reader) can quickly pick out the questions relevant to your goals, answer them for your microservice, and then determine what steps you can take to make your microservice production-ready. At the end of the book, you will find two appendixes (Appendix A, *Production-Readiness Checklist*, and Appendix B, *Evaluate Your Microservice*) that will help you keep track of the production-readiness standards and the "Evaluate Your Microservices" questions that are scattered throughout the book.

How This Book Is Structured

As the title suggests, Chapter 1, *Microservices*, is an introduction to microservices. It covers the basics of microservice architecture, covers some of the details of splitting a monolith into microservices, introduces the four layers of a microservice ecosystem, and concludes with a section devoted to illuminating some of the organizational challenges and trade-offs that come with adopting microservice architecture.

In Chapter 2, *Production-Readiness*, the challenges of microservice standardization are presented, and the eight production-readiness standards, all driven by microservice availability, are introduced.

Chapter 3, *Stability and Reliability*, is all about the principles of building stable and reliable microservices. The development cycle, deployment pipeline, dealing with dependencies, routing and discovery, and stable and reliable deprecation and decommissioning of microservices are all covered here.

Chapter 4, *Scalability and Performance*, narrows in on the requirements for building scalable and performant microservices, including knowing the growth scales of microservices, using resources efficiently, being resource aware, capacity planning, dependency scaling, traffic management, task handling and processing, and scalable data storage.

Chapter 5, *Fault Tolerance and Catastrophe-Preparedness*, covers the principles of building fault-tolerant microservices that are prepared for any catastrophe, including common catastrophes and failure scenarios, strategies for failure detection and remediation, the ins and outs of resiliency testing, and ways to handle incidents and outages.

Chapter 6, *Monitoring*, is all about the nitty-gritty details of microservice monitoring and how to avoid the complexities of microservice monitoring through standardization. Logging, creating useful dashboards, and appropriately handling alerting are all covered in this chapter.

Last but not least is Chapter 7, *Documentation and Understanding*, which dives into appropriate microservice documentation and ways to increase architectural and operational understanding in development teams and throughout the organization, and also contains practical strategies for implementing production-readiness standards across an engineering organization.

There are two appendixes at the end of this book. Appendix A, *Production-Readiness Checklist*, is the checklist described at the end of Chapter 7, *Documentation and Understanding*, and is a concise summary of all the production-readiness standards that are scattered throughout the book, along with their corresponding requirements. Appendix B, *Evaluate Your Microservice*, is a collection of all the "Evaluate Your

Microservice" questions found in the corresponding sections at the end of Chapters 3-7.

Conventions Used in This Book

The following typographical conventions are used in this book:

Italic
> Indicates new terms, URLs, email addresses, filenames, and file extensions.

`Constant width`
> Used for program listings, as well as within paragraphs to refer to program elements such as variable or function names, databases, data types, environment variables, statements, and keywords.

`Constant width bold`
> Shows commands or other text that should be typed literally by the user.

`Constant width italic`
> Shows text that should be replaced with user-supplied values or by values determined by context.

> This element signifies a tip or suggestion.

> This element signifies a general note.

> This element indicates a warning or caution.

O'Reilly Safari

 *Safari* (formerly Safari Books Online) is a membership-based training and reference platform for enterprise, government, educators, and individuals.

Members have access to thousands of books, training videos, Learning Paths, interactive tutorials, and curated playlists from over 250 publishers, including O'Reilly Media, Harvard Business Review, Prentice Hall Professional, Addison-Wesley Professional, Microsoft Press, Sams, Que, Peachpit Press, Adobe, Focal Press, Cisco Press, John Wiley & Sons, Syngress, Morgan Kaufmann, IBM Redbooks, Packt, Adobe Press, FT Press, Apress, Manning, New Riders, McGraw-Hill, Jones & Bartlett, and Course Technology, among others.

For more information, please visit *http://oreilly.com/safari*.

How to Contact Us

Please address comments and questions concerning this book to the publisher:

O'Reilly Media, Inc.
1005 Gravenstein Highway North
Sebastopol, CA 95472
800-998-9938 (in the United States or Canada)
707-829-0515 (international or local)
707-829-0104 (fax)

We have a web page for this book, where we list errata, examples, and any additional information. You can access this page at *http://bit.ly/prod-ready_microservices*.

To comment or ask technical questions about this book, send email to *bookquestions@oreilly.com*.

For more information about our books, courses, conferences, and news, see our website at *http://www.oreilly.com*.

Find us on Facebook: *http://facebook.com/oreilly*

Follow us on Twitter: *http://twitter.com/oreillymedia*

Watch us on YouTube: *http://www.youtube.com/oreillymedia*

Acknowledgments

This book is dedicated to my better half, Chad Rigetti, who took time away from building quantum computers to listen to all of my rants about microservices, and who joyfully encouraged me every step of the way. I could not have written this book without all of his love and wholehearted support.

It is also dedicated to my sisters, Martha and Sara, whose grit, resilience, courage, and joy inspire me in every moment and aspect of my life, and also to Shalon Van Tine, who has been my closest friend and fiercest supporter for so many years.

I am greatly indebted to all of those who offered feedback on early drafts, to my coworkers at Uber, and to engineers who have bravely worked to implement the principles and strategies within this book at their own engineering organizations. I am especially thankful to Roxana del Toro, Patrick Schork, Rick Boone, Tyler Dixon, Jonah Horowitz, Ryan Rix, Katherine Hennes, Ingrid Avendano, Sean Hart, Shella Stephens, David Campbell, Jameson Lee, Jane Arc, Eamon Bisson-Donahue, and Aimee Gonzalez.

None of this would have been possible without Brian Foster, Nan Barber, the technical reviewers, and the rest of the amazing O'Reilly staff. I could not have written this without you.

CHAPTER 1

Microservices

In the past few years, the technology industry has witnessed a rapid change in applied, practical distributed systems architecture that has led industry giants (such as Netflix, Twitter, Amazon, eBay, and Uber) away from building monolithic applications to adopting microservice architecture. While the fundamental concepts behind microservices are not new, the contemporary application of microservice architecture truly is, and its adoption has been driven in part by scalability challenges, lack of efficiency, slow developer velocity, and the difficulties with adopting new technologies that arise when complex software systems are contained within and deployed as one large monolithic application.

Adopting microservice architecture, whether from the ground up or by splitting an existing monolithic application into independently developed and deployed microservices, solves these problems. With microservice architecture, an application can easily be scaled both horizontally and vertically, developer productivity and velocity increase dramatically, and old technologies can easily be swapped out for the newest ones.

As we will see in this chapter, the adoption of microservice architecture can be seen as a natural step in the scaling of an application. The splitting of a monolithic application into microservices is driven by scalability and efficiency concerns, but microservices introduce challenges of their own. A successful, scalable microservice ecosystem requires that a stable and sophisticated infrastructure be in place. In addition, the organizational structure of a company adopting microservices must be radically changed to support microservice architecture, and the team structures that spring from this can lead to siloing and sprawl. The largest challenges that microservice architecture brings, however, are the need for standardization of the architecture of the services themselves, along with requirements for each microservice in order to ensure trust and availability.

From Monoliths to Microservices

Almost every software application written today can be broken into three distinct elements: a *frontend* (or *client-side*) piece, a *backend* piece, and some type of *datastore* (Figure 1-1). Requests are made to the application through the client-side piece, the backend code does all the heavy lifting, and any relevant data that needs to be stored or accessed (whether temporarily in memory of permanently in a database) is sent to or retrieved from wherever the data is stored. We'll call this *the three-tier architecture*.

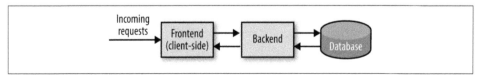

Figure 1-1. Three-tier architecture

There are three different ways these elements can be combined to make an application. Most applications put the first two pieces into one codebase (or repository), where all client-side and backend code are stored and run as one executable file, with a separate database. Others separate out all frontend, client-side code from the backend code and store them as separate logical executables, accompanied by an external database. Applications that don't require an external database and store all data in memory tend to combine all three elements into one repository. Regardless of the way these elements are divided or combined, the *application* itself is considered to be the sum of these three distinct elements.

Applications are usually architected, built, and run this way from the beginning of their lifecycles, and the architecture of the application is typically independent of the product offered by the company or the purpose of the application itself. These three architectural elements that comprise the three-tier architecture are present in every website, every phone application, every backend and frontend and strange enormous enterprise application, and are found as one of the permutations described.

In the early stages, when a company is young, its application(s) simple, and the number of developers contributing to the codebase is small, developers typically share the burden of contributing to and maintaining the codebase. As the company grows, more developers are hired, new features are added to the application, and three significant things happen.

First comes an increase in the operational workload. Operational work is, generally speaking, the work associated with running and maintaining the application. This usually leads to the hiring of operational engineers (system administrators, TechOps engineers, and so-called "DevOps" engineers) who take over the majority of the operational tasks, like those related to hardware, monitoring, and on call.

The second thing that happens is a result of simple mathematics: adding new features to your application increases both the number of lines of code in your application and the complexity of the application itself.

Third is the necessary horizontal and/or vertical scaling of the application. Increases in traffic place significant scalability and performance demands on the application, requiring that more servers host the application. More servers are added, a copy of the application is deployed to each server, and load balancers are put into place so that the requests are distributed appropriately among the servers hosting the application (see Figure 1-2, containing a frontend piece, which may contain its own load-balancing layer, a backend load-balancing layer, and the backend servers). Vertical scaling becomes a necessity as the application begins processing a larger number of tasks related to its diverse set of features, so the application is deployed to larger, more powerful servers that can handle CPU and memory demands (Figure 1-3).

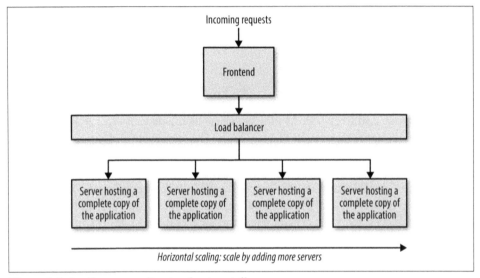

Figure 1-2. Scaling an application horizontally

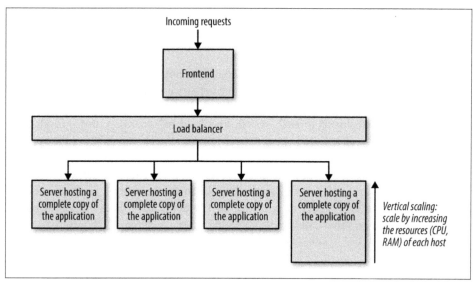

Figure 1-3. Scaling an application vertically

As the company grows, and the number of engineers is no longer in the single, double, or even triple digits, things start to get a little more complicated. Thanks to all the features, patches, and fixes added to the codebase by the developers, the application is now thousands upon thousands of lines long. The complexity of the application is growing steadily, and hundreds (if not thousands) of tests must be written in order to ensure that any change made (even a change of one or two lines) doesn't compromise the integrity of the existing thousands upon thousands of lines of code. Development and deployment become a nightmare, testing becomes a burden and a blocker to the deployment of even the most crucial fixes, and technical debt piles up quickly. Applications whose lifecycles fit into this pattern (for better or for worse) are fondly (and appropriately) referred to in the software community as *monoliths*.

Of course, not all monolithic applications are bad, and not every monolithic application suffers from the problems listed, but monoliths that don't hit these issues at some point in their lifecycle are (in my experience) pretty rare. The reason most monoliths are susceptible to these problems is because the nature of a monolith is directly opposed to *scalability* in the most general possible sense. Scalability requires *concurrency* and *partitioning*: the two things that are difficult to accomplish with a monolith.

Scaling an Application

Let's break this down a bit.

The goal of any software application is to process tasks of some sort. Regardless of what those tasks are, we can make a general assumption about how we want our application to handle them: it needs to process them efficiently.

To process tasks efficiently, our application needs to have some kind of *concurrency*. This means that we can't have just one process that does all the work, because then that process will pick up one task at a time, complete all the necessary pieces of it (or fail!), and then move onto the next—this isn't efficient at all! To make our application efficient, we can introduce concurrency so that each task can be broken up into smaller pieces.

The second thing we can do to process tasks efficiently is to divide and conquer by introducing *partitioning*, where each task is not only broken up into small pieces but can be processed in parallel. If we have a bunch of tasks, we can process them all at the same time by sending them to a set of workers that can process them in parallel. If we need to process more tasks, we can easily scale with the demand by adding additional workers to process the new tasks without affecting the efficiency of our system.

Concurrency and partitioning are difficult to support when you have one large application that needs to be deployed to every server, which needs to process any type of task. If your application is even the slightest bit complicated, the only way you can scale it with a growing list of features and increasing traffic is to scale up the hardware that the application is deployed to.

To be truly efficient, the best way to scale an application is to break it into many small, independent applications that each do one type of task. Need to add another step to the overall process? Easy enough: just make a new application that only does that step! Need to handle more traffic? Simple: add more workers to each application!

Concurrency and partitioning are difficult to support in a monolithic application, which prevents monolithic application architecture from being as efficient as we need it to be.

We've seen this pattern emerge at companies like Amazon, Twitter, Netflix, eBay, and Uber: companies that run applications across not hundreds, but thousands, even hundreds of thousands of servers and whose applications have evolved into monoliths and hit scalability challenges. The challenges they faced were remedied by abandoning monolithic application architecture in favor of *microservices*.

The basic concept of a microservice is simple: it's a small application that does one thing only, and does that one thing well. A microservice is a small component that is easily replaceable, independently developed, and independently deployable. A micro-service cannot live alone, however—no microservice is an island—and it is part of a larger system, running and working alongside other microservices to accomplish what would normally be handled by one large standalone application.

The goal of microservice architecture is to build a set of small applications that are each responsible for performing one function (as opposed to the traditional way of building one application that does everything), and to let each microservice be autonomous, independent, and self-contained. The core difference between a monolithic application and microservices is this: a monolithic application (Figure 1-4) will contain all features and functions within one application and one codebase, all deployed at the same time, with each server hosting a complete copy of the entire application, while a microservice (Figure 1-5) contains only one function or feature and lives in a *microservice ecosystem* along with other microservices that each perform one function or feature.

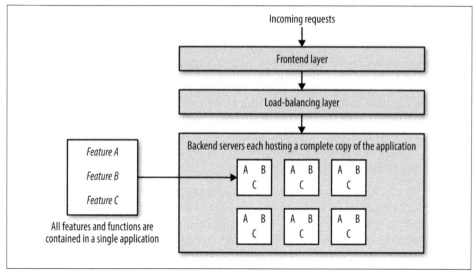

Figure 1-4. Monolith

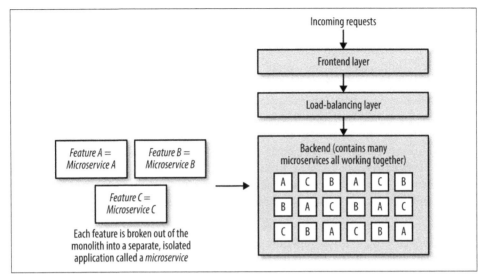

Figure 1-5. Microservices

There are numerous benefits to adopting microservice architecture—including (but not limited to) reduced technical debt, improved developer productivity and velocity, better testing efficiency, increased scalability, and ease of deployment—and companies that adopt microservice architecture usually do so after having built one application and hitting scalability and organizational challenges. They begin with a monolithic application and then *split the monolith* into microservices.

The difficulties of splitting a monolith into microservices depend entirely on the complexity of the monolithic application. A monolithic application with many features will take a great deal of architectural effort and careful deliberation to successfully break up into microservices, and additional complexity is introduced by the need to reorganize and restructure teams. The decision to move to microservices must always become a company-wide effort.

There are several steps in breaking apart a monolith. The first is to identify the components that should be written as independent services. This is perhaps the most difficult step in the entire process, because while there may be a number of right ways to split the monolith into component services, there are far more wrong ways. The rule of thumb in identifying components is to pinpoint key overall functionalities of the monolith, then split those functionalities into small independent components. Microservices must be as simple as possible or else the company will risk the possibility of replacing one monolith with several smaller monoliths, which will all suffer the same problems as the company grows.

Once the key functions have been identified and properly componentized into independent microservices, the organizational structure of the company must be restructured so that each microservice is staffed by an engineering team. There are several ways to do this. The first method of company reorganization around microservice adoption is to dedicate one team to each microservice. The size of the team will be determined completely by the complexity and workload of the microservice and should be staffed by enough developers and site reliability engineers so that both feature development and the on-call rotation of the service can be managed without burdening the team. The second is to assign several services to one team and have that team develop the services in parallel. This works best when the teams are organized around specific products or business domains, and are responsible for developing any services related to those products or domains. If a company chooses the second method of reorganization, it needs to make sure that developers aren't overworked and don't face task, outage, or operational fatigue.

Another important part of microservice adoption is the creation of a *microservice ecosystem*. Typically (or, at least, hopefully), a company running a large monolithic application will have a dedicated infrastructure organization that is responsible for designing, building, and maintaining the infrastructure that the application runs on. When a monolith is split into microservices, the responsibilities of the infrastructure organization for providing a stable platform for microservices to be developed and run on grows drastically in importance. The infrastructure teams must provide microservice teams with stable infrastructure that abstracts away the majority of the complexity of the interactions between microservices.

Once these three steps have been completed—the componentization of the application, the restructuring of engineering teams to staff each microservice, and the development of the infrastructure organization within the company—the migration can begin. Some teams choose to pull the relevant code for their microservice directly from the monolith and into a separate service, and shadow the monolith's traffic until they are convinced that the microservice can perform the desired functionality on its own. Other teams choose to build the service from scratch, starting with a clean slate, and shadow traffic or redirect after the service has passed appropriate tests. The best approach to migration depends on the functionality of the microservice, and I have seen both approaches work equally well in most cases, but the real key to a successful migration is thorough, careful, painstakingly documented planning and execution, along with the realization that a complete migration of a large monolith can take several long years.

With all the work involved in splitting a monolith into microservices, it may seem better to begin with microservice architecture, skip all of the painful scalability challenges, and avoid the microservice migration drama. This approach may turn out all right for some companies, but I want to offer several words of caution. Small companies often do not have the necessary infrastructure in place to sustain microservices, even at a very small scale: good microservice architecture requires stable, often very complex, infrastructure. Such stable infrastructure requires a large, dedicated team whose cost can typically be sustained only by companies that have reached the scalability challenges that justify the move to microservice architecture. Small companies simply will not have enough operational capacity to maintain a microservice ecosystem. Furthermore, it's extraordinarily difficult to identify key areas and components to build into microservices when a company is in the early stages: applications at new companies will not have many features, nor many separate areas of functionality that can be split appropriately into microservices.

Microservice Architecture

The *architecture of a microservice* (Figure 1-6) is not very different from the standard application architecture covered in the first section of this chapter (Figure 1-1). Each and every microservice will have three components: a frontend (client-side) piece, some backend code that does the heavy lifting, and a way to store or retrieve any relevant data.

The frontend, client-side piece of a microservice is not your typical frontend application, but rather an *application programming interface* (API) with static *endpoints*. Well-designed microservice APIs allow microservices to easily and effectively interact, sending requests to the relevant API endpoint(s). For example, a microservice that is responsible for customer data might have a *get_customer_information* endpoint that other services could send requests to in order to retrieve information about customers, an *update_customer_information* endpoint that other services could send requests to in order to update the information for a specific customer, and a *delete_customer_information* endpoint that services could use to delete a customer's information.

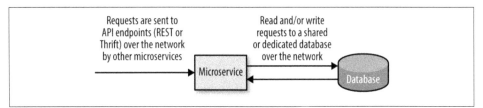

Figure 1-6. Elements of microservice architecture

These endpoints are separated out in architecture and theory alone, not in practice, for they live alongside and as part of all the backend code that processes every request. For our example microservice that is responsible for customer data, a request sent to the *get_customer_information* endpoint would trigger a task that would process the incoming request, determine any specific filters or options that were applied in the request, retrieve the information from a database, format the information, and return it to the client (microservice) that requested it.

Most microservices will store some type of data, whether in memory (perhaps using a cache) or an external database. If the relevant data is stored in memory, there's no need to make an extra network call to an external database, and the microservice can easily return any relevant data to a client. If the data is stored in an external database, the microservice will need to make another request to the database, wait for a response, and then continue to process the task.

This architecture is necessary if microservices are to work well together. The micro-service architecture paradigm requires that a set of microservices work together to make up what would otherwise exist as one large application, and so there are certain elements of this architecture that need to be standardized across an entire organiza-tion if a set of microservices is to interact successfully and efficiently.

The API endpoints of microservices should be standardized across an organization. That is not to say that all microservices should have the same specific endpoints, but that the type of endpoint should be the same. Two very common types of API end-points for microservices are REST or Apache Thrift, and I've seen some microservi-ces that have both types of endpoints (though this is rare, makes monitoring rather complicated, and I don't particularly recommend it). Choice of endpoint type is reflective of the internal workings of the microservice itself, and will also dictate its architecture: it's difficult to build an asynchronous microservice that communicates via HTTP over REST endpoints, for example, which would necessitate adding a messaging-based endpoint to the services as well.

Microservices interact with each other via *remote procedure calls* (RPCs), which are calls over the network designed to look and behave exactly like local procedure calls. The protocols used will be dependent on architectural choices and organizational support, as well as the endpoints used. A microservice with REST endpoints, for example, will likely interact with other microservices via HTTP, while a microservice with Thrift endpoints may communicate with other microservices over HTTP or a more customized, in-house solution.

Avoid Versioning Microservices and Endpoints

A microservice is not a library (it is not loaded into memory at compilation-time or during runtime) but an independent software application. Due to the fast-paced nature of microservice develop-ment, versioning microservices can easily become an organiza-tional nightmare, with developers on client services pinning specific (outdated, unmaintained) versions of a microservice in their own code. Microservices should be treated as living, changing things, not static releases or libraries. Versioning of API endpoints is another anti-pattern that should be avoided for the same reasons.

Any type of endpoint and any protocol used to communicate with other microservices will have benefits and trade-offs. The architectural decisions here shouldn't be made by the individual developer who is building a microservice, but should be part of the architectural design of the microservice ecosystem as a whole (we'll get to this in the next section).

Writing a microservice gives the developer a great deal of freedom: aside from any organizational choices regarding API endpoints and communication protocols, developers are free to write the internal workings of their microservice however they wish. It can be written in any language whatsoever—it can be written in Go, in Java, in Erlang, in Haskell—as long as the endpoints and communication protocols are taken care of. Developing a microservice is not all that different from developing a standalone application. There are some caveats to this, as we will see in the final section of this chapter ("Organizational Challenges" on page 20), because developer freedom with regard to language choice comes at a hefty cost to the engineering organization.

In this way, a microservice can be treated by others as a black box: you put some information in by sending a request to one of its endpoints, and you get something out. If you get what you want and need out of the microservice in a reasonable time and without any crazy errors, it has done its job, and there's no need to understand anything further than the endpoints you need to hit and whether or not the service is working properly.

Our discussion of the specifics of microservice architecture will end here—not because this is all there is to microservice architecture, but because each of the following chapters within this book is devoted to bringing microservices to this ideal black-box state.

The Microservice Ecosystem

Microservices do not live in isolation. The environment in which microservices are built, are run, and interact is where they *live*. The complexities of the large-scale microservice environment are on par with the ecological complexities of a rainforest, a desert, or an ocean, and considering this environment as an ecosystem—a *microservice ecosystem*—is beneficial in adopting microservice architecture.

In well-designed, sustainable microservice ecosystems, the microservices are abstracted away from all infrastructure. They are abstracted away from the hardware, abstracted away from the networks, abstracted away from the build and deployment pipeline, abstracted away from service discovery and load balancing. This is all part of the infrastructure of the microservice ecosystem, and building, standardizing, and maintaining this infrastructure in a stable, scalable, fault-tolerant, and reliable way is essential for successful microservice operation.

The infrastructure has to sustain the microservice ecosystem. The goal of all infrastructure engineers and architects must be to remove the low-level operational concerns from microservice development and build a stable infrastructure that can scale, one that developers can easily build and run microservices on top of. Developing a microservice within a stable microservice ecosystem should be just like developing a small standalone application. This requires very sophisticated, top-notch infrastructure.

The microservice ecosystem can be split into four layers (Figure 1-7), though the boundaries of each are not always clearly defined: some elements of the infrastructure will touch every part of the stack. The lower three layers are the infrastructure layers: at the bottom of the stack we find the hardware layer, and on top of that, the communication layer (which bleeds up into the fourth layer), followed by the application platform. The fourth (top) layer is where all individual microservices live.

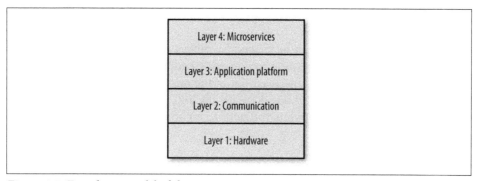

Figure 1-7. Four-layer model of the microservice ecosystem

Layer 1: Hardware

At the very bottom of the microservice ecosystem, we find the *hardware layer*. These are the actual machines, the real, physical computers that all internal tools and all microservices run on. These servers are located on racks within datacenters, being cooled by expensive HVAC systems and powered by electricity. Many different types of servers can live here: some are optimized for databases; others for processing CPU-intensive tasks. These servers can either be owned by the company itself, or "rented" from so-called cloud providers like Amazon Web Services' Elastic Compute Cloud (AWS EC2), Google Cloud Platform (GCP), or Microsoft Azure.

The choice of specific hardware is determined by the owners of the servers. If your company is running your own datacenters, the choice of hardware is your own, and you can optimize the server choice for your specific needs. If you are running servers in the cloud (which is the more common scenario), your choice is limited to whatever hardware is offered by the cloud provider. Choosing between *bare metal* and a *cloud provider* (or providers) is not an easy decision to make, and cost, availability, reliability, and operational expenses are things that need to be considered.

Managing these servers is part of the hardware layer. Each server needs to have an *operating system* installed, and the operating system should be standardized across all servers. There is no correct, right answer as to which operating system a microservice ecosystem should use: the answer to this question depends entirely on the applications you will be building, the languages they will be written in, and the libraries and tools that your microservices require. The majority of microservice ecosystems run some variant of Linux, commonly CentOS, Debian, or Ubuntu, but a .NET company will, obviously, choose differently. Additional abstractions can be built and layered atop the hardware: resource isolation and resource abstraction (as offered by technologies like Docker and Apache Mesos) also belong in this layer, as do databases (dedicated or shared).

Installing an operating system and *provisioning* the hardware is the first layer on top of the servers themselves. Each host must be provisioned and configured, and after the operating system is installed, a *configuration management* tool (such as Ansible, Chef, or Puppet) should be used to install all of the applications and set all the necessary configurations.

The hosts need proper *host-level monitoring* (using something like Nagios) and *host-level logging* so that if anything happens (disk failure, network failure, or if CPU utilization goes through the roof), problems with the hosts can be easily diagnosed, mitigated, and resolved. Host-level monitoring is covered in greater detail in Chapter 6, *Monitoring*.

Summary of Layer 1: The Hardware Layer

The hardware layer (layer 1) of the microservice ecosystem contains:

- The physical servers (owned by the company or rented from cloud providers)
- Databases (dedicated and/or shared)
- The operating system
- Resource isolation and abstraction
- Configuration management
- Host-level monitoring
- Host-level logging

Layer 2: Communication

The second layer of the microservice ecosystem is the *communication layer*. The communication layer bleeds into all of the other layers of the ecosystem (including the application platform and microservices layers), because it is where all communication between services is handled; the boundaries between the communication layer and each other layer of the microservice ecosystem are poorly defined. While the boundaries may not be clear, the elements *are* clear: the second layer of a microservice ecosystem always contains the network, DNS, RPCs and API endpoints, service discovery, service registry, and load balancing.

Discussing the network and DNS elements of the communication layer is beyond the scope of this book, so we will be focusing on RPCs, API endpoints, service discovery, service registry, and load balancing in this section.

RPCs, endpoints, and messaging

Microservices interact with one another over the network using *remote procedure calls* (RPCs) or *messaging* to the *API endpoints* of other microservices (or, as we will see in the case of messaging, to a message broker which will route the message appropriately). The basic idea is this: using a specified protocol, a microservice will send some data in a standardized format over the network to another service (perhaps to another microservice's API endpoint) or to a message broker which will make sure that the data is send to another microservice's API endpoint.

There are several microservice communication paradigms. The first is the most common: *HTTP+REST/THRIFT*. In HTTP+REST/THRIFT, services communicate with each other over the network using the *Hypertext Transfer Protocol* (HTTP), and sending requests and receiving responses to or from either specific *representational state transfer* (REST) endpoints (using various methods, like GET, POST, etc.) or specific *Apache Thrift* endpoints (or both). The data is usually formatted and sent as *JSON* (or *protocol buffers*) over HTTP.

HTTP+REST is the most convenient form of microservice communication. There aren't any surprises, it's easy to set up, and is the most stable and reliable—mostly because it's difficult to implement incorrectly. The downside of adopting this paradigm is that it is, by necessity, synchronous (blocking).

The second communication paradigm is *messaging*. Messaging is asynchronous (non-blocking), but it's a bit more complicated. Messaging works the following way: a microservice will send data (a *message*) over the network (HTTP or other) to a *message broker*, which will route the communication to other microservices.

Messaging comes in several flavors, the two most popular being *publish–subscribe* (pubsub) messaging and *request–response* messaging. In pubsub models, clients will *subscribe* to a *topic* and will receive a message whenever a *publisher publishes* a message to that topic. Request–response models are more straightforward, where a client will send a *request* to a service (or message broker), which will *respond* with the information requested. There are some messaging technologies that are a unique blend of both models, like Apache Kafka. Celery and Redis (or Celery with RabbitMQ) can be used for messaging (and task processing) for microservices written in Python: Celery processes the tasks and/or messages using Redis or RabbitMQ as the broker.

Messaging comes with several significant downsides that must be mitigated. Messaging can be just as scalable (if not more scalable) than HTTP+REST solutions, if it is architected for scalability from the get-go. Inherently, messaging is not as easy to change and update, and its centralized nature (while it may seem like a benefit) can lead to its queues and brokers becoming points of failure for the entire ecosystem. The asynchronous nature of messaging can lead to race conditions and endless loops if not prepared for. If a messaging system is implemented with protections against these problems, it can become as stable and efficient as a synchronous solution.

Service discovery, service registry, and load balancing

In monolithic architecture, traffic only needs to be sent to one application and distributed appropriately to the servers hosting the application. In microservice architecture, traffic needs to be routed appropriately to a large number of different applications, and then distributed appropriately to the servers hosting each specific microservice. In order for this to be done efficiently and effectively, microservice architecture requires three technologies be implemented in the communication layer: *service discovery*, *service registry*, and *load balancing*.

In general, when a microservice A needs to make a request to another microservice B, microservice A needs to know the IP address and port of a specific instance where microservice B is hosted. More specifically, the communication layer between the microservices needs to know the IP addresses and ports of these microservices so that the requests between them can be routed appropriately. This is accomplished through *service discovery* (such as etcd, Consul, Hyperbahn, or ZooKeeper), which ensures that requests are routed to exactly where they are supposed to be sent and that (very importantly) they are only routed to healthy instances. Service discovery requires a *service registry*, which is a database that tracks all ports and IPs of all microservices across the ecosystem.

Dynamic Scaling and Assigned Ports

In microservice architecture, ports and IPs can (and do) change all of the time, especially as microservices are scaled and re-deployed (especially with a hardware abstraction layer like Apache Mesos). One way to approach the discovery and routing is to assign static ports (both frontend and backend) to each microservice.

Unless you have each microservice hosted on only one instance (which is highly unlikely), you'll need *load balancing* in place in various parts of the communication layer across the microservice ecosystem. Load balancing works, at a very high level, like this: if you have 10 different instances hosting a microservice, load-balancing software (and/or hardware) will ensure that the traffic is distributed (balanced) across all of the instances. Load balancing will be needed at every location in the ecosystem in which a request is being sent to an application, which means that any large microservice ecosystem will contain many, many layers of load balancing. Commonly used load balancers for this purpose are Amazon Web Services Elastic Load Balancer, Netflix Eureka, HAProxy, and Nginx.

Summary of Layer 2: The Communication Layer

The communication layer (layer 2) of the microservice ecosystem contains:

- Network
- DNS
- Remote procedure calls (RPCs)
- Endpoints
- Messaging
- Service discovery
- Service registry
- Load balancing

Layer 3: The Application Platform

The *application platform* is the third layer of the microservice ecosystem and contains all of the internal tooling and services that are independent of the microservices. This layer is filled with centralized, ecosystem-wide tools and services that must be built in such a way that microservice development teams do not have to design, build, or maintain anything except their own microservices.

A good application platform is one with *self-service internal tools* for developers, a standardized *development process*, a centralized and automated *build and release system*, *automated testing*, a standardized and centralized *deployment solution*, and centralized *logging and microservice-level monitoring*. Many of the details of these elements are covered in later chapters, but we'll cover several of them briefly here to provide some introduction to the basic concepts.

Self-service internal development tools

Quite a few things can be categorized as *self-service internal development tools*, and which particular things fall into this category depends not only on the needs of the developers, but the level of abstraction and sophistication of both the infrastructure and the ecosystem as a whole. The key to determining which tools need to be built is to first divide the realms of responsibility and then determine which tasks developers need to be able to accomplish in order to design, build, and maintain their services.

Within a company that has adopted microservice architecture, responsibilities need to be carefully delegated to different engineering teams. An easy way to do this is to create an engineering suborganization for each layer of the microservice ecosystem, along with other teams that bridge each layer. Each of these engineering organizations, functioning semi-independently, will be responsible for everything within their layer: TechOps teams will be responsible for layer 1, infrastructure teams will be responsible for layer 2, application platform teams will be responsible for layer 3, and microservice teams will be responsible for layer 4 (this is, of course, a very simplified view, but you get the general idea).

Within this organizational scheme, any time that an engineer working on one of the higher layers needs to set up, configure, or utilize something on one of the lower layers, there should be a self-service tool in place that the engineer can use. For example, the team working on messaging for the ecosystem should build a self-service tool so that if a developer on a microservice team needs to configure messaging for her service, she can easily configure the messaging without having to understand all of the intricacies of the messaging system.

There are many reasons to have these centralized, self-service tools in place for each layer. In a diverse microservice ecosystem, the average engineer on any given team will have no (or very little) knowledge of how the services and systems in other teams work, and there is simply no way they could become experts in each service and system while working on their own—it simply can't be done. Each individual developer will know almost nothing except her own service, but together, all of the developers working within the ecosystem will collectively know everything. Rather than trying to educate each developer about the intricacies of each tool and service within the ecosystem, build sustainable, easy-to-use user interfaces for every part of the ecosystem, and then educate and train them on how to use those. Turn everything into a black box, and document exactly how it works and how to use it.

The second reason to build these tools and build them well is that, in all honesty, you do not want a developer from another team to be able to make significant changes to your service or system, especially not one that could cause an outage. This is especially true and compelling for services and systems belonging to the lower layers (layer 1, layer 2, and layer 3). Allowing nonexperts to make changes to things within these layers, or requiring (or worse, expecting) them to become experts in these areas is a recipe for disaster. An example of where this can go terribly wrong is in configuration management: allowing developers on microservice teams to make changes to system configurations without having the expertise to do so can and will lead to large-scale production outages if a change is made that affects something other than their service alone.

The development cycle

When developers are making changes to existing microservices, or creating new ones, development can be made more effective by streamlining and standardizing the development process and automating away as much as possible. The details of standardizing the process of stable and reliable development itself are covered in Chapter 4, *Scalability and Performance*, but there are several things that need to be in place within the third layer of a microservice ecosystem in order for stable and reliable development to be possible.

The first requirement is a centralized *version control system* where all code can be stored, tracked, versioned, and searched. This is usually accomplished through something like GitHub, or a self-hosted git or svn repository linked to some kind of collaboration tool like Phabrictor, and these tools make it easy to maintain and review code.

The second requirement is a stable, efficient *development environment*. Development environments are notoriously difficult to implement in microservice ecosystems, due to the complicated dependencies each microservice will have on other services, but they are absolutely essential. Some engineering organizations prefer when all development is done locally (on a developer's laptop), but this can lead to bad deploys because it doesn't give the developer an accurate picture of how her code changes will perform in the production world. The most stable and reliable way to design a development environment is to create a mirror of the production environment (one that is not staging, nor canary, nor production) containing all of the intricate dependency chains.

Test, build, package, and release

The *test, build, package, and release steps* in between development and deployment should be standardized and centralized as much as possible. After the development cycle, when any code change has been committed, all the necessary tests should be run, and new releases should be automatically built and packaged. *Continuous integration* tooling exists for precisely this purpose, and existing solutions (like Jenkins) are very advanced and easy to configure. These tools make it easy to automate the entire process, leaving very little room for human error.

Deployment pipeline

The *deployment pipeline* is the process by which new code makes its way to production servers after the development cycle and following the test, build, package, and release steps. Deployment can quickly become very complicated in a microservice ecosystem, where hundreds of deployments per day are not out of the ordinary. Building tooling around deployment, and standardizing deployment practices for all development teams is often necessary. The principles of building stable and reliable (production-ready) deployment pipelines are covered in detail in Chapter 3, *Stability and Reliability*.

Logging and monitoring

All microservices should have *microservice-level logging* of all requests made to the microservice (including all relevant and important information) and its responses. Due to the fast-paced nature of microservice development, it's often impossible to reproduce bugs in the code because it's impossible to reconstruct the state of the system at the time of failure. Good microservice-level logging gives developers the information they need to fully understand the state of their service at a certain time in the past or present. *Microservice-level monitoring* of all *key metrics* of the microservices is essential for similar reasons: accurate, real-time monitoring allows developers to always know the health and status of their service. Microservice-level logging and monitoring are covered in greater detail in Chapter 6, *Monitoring*.

Summary of Layer 3: The Application Platform Layer

The application platform layer (layer 3) of the microservice ecosystem contains:

- Self-service internal development tools
- Development environment
- Test, package, build, and release tools
- Deployment pipeline
- Microservice-level logging
- Microservice-level monitoring

Layer 4: Microservices

At the very top of the microservice ecosystem lies the *microservice layer* (*layer 4*). This layer is where the microservices—and anything specific to them—live, completely abstracted away from the lower infrastructure layers. Here they are abstracted from the hardware, from deployment, from service discovery, from load balancing, and from communication. The only things that are not abstracted away from the microservice layer are the configurations specific to each service for using the tools.

It is common practice in software engineering to centralize all application configurations so that the configurations for a specific tool or set of tools (like configuration management, resource isolation, or deployment tools) are all stored with the tool itself. For example, custom deployment configurations for applications are often stored not with the application code but with the code for the deployment tool. This practice works well for monolithic architecture, and even for small microservice ecosystems, but in very large microservice ecosystems containing hundreds of microservices and dozens of internal tools (each with their own custom configurations), this practice becomes rather messy: developers on microservice teams are required to make changes to codebases of tools in the layers below, and oftentimes will forget where certain configurations live (or that they exist at all). To mitigate this problem, all microservice-specific configurations can live in the repository of the microservice and should be accessed there by the tools and systems of the layers below.

Summary of Layer 4: The Microservice Layer

The microservice layer (layer 4) of the microservice ecosystem contains:

- The microservices
- All microservice-specific configurations

Organizational Challenges

The adoption of microservice architecture resolves the most pressing challenges presented by monolithic application architecture. Microservices aren't plagued by the same scalability challenges, the lack of efficiency, or the difficulties in adopting new technologies: they are optimized for scalability, optimized for efficiency, optimized for developer velocity. In an industry where new technologies rapidly gain market traction, the pure organizational cost of maintaining and attempting to improve a cumbersome monolithic application is simply not practical. With these things in mind, it's hard to imagine why anyone would be reluctant to split a monolith into microservices, why anyone would be wary about building a microservice ecosystem from the ground up.

Microservices seem like a magical (and somewhat obvious) solution, but we know better than that. In *The Mythical Man-Month*, Frederick Brooks explained why there are no silver bullets in software engineering, an idea he summarized as follows: "There is no single development, in either technology or management technique, which by itself promises even one order-of-magnitude improvement within a decade in productivity, in reliability, in simplicity."

When we find ourselves presented with technology that promises to offer us drastic improvements, we need to look for the trade-offs. Microservices promise greater scalability and greater efficiency, but we know that those will come at a cost to some part of the overall system.

There are four especially significant trade-offs that come with microservice architecture. The first is the change in organizational structure that tends toward isolation and poor cross-team communication—a consequence of the inverse of *Conway's Law*. The second is the dramatic increase in *technical sprawl*, sprawl that is extraordinarily costly not only to the entire organization but which also presents significant costs to each engineer. The third trade-off is the increased *ability of the system to fail*. The fourth is the *competition for engineering and infrastructure resources*.

The Inverse Conway's Law

The idea behind *Conway's Law* (named after programmer Melvin Conway in 1968) is this: that the architecture of a system will be determined by the communication and organizational structures of the company. The inverse of Conway's Law (which we'll call the *Inverse Conway's Law*) is also valid and is especially relevant to the microservice ecosystem: the organizational structure of a company is determined by the architecture of its product. Over 40 years after Conway's Law was first introduced, both it and its inverse still appear to hold true. Microsoft's organizational structure, if sketched out as if it were the architecture of a system, looks remarkably like the architecture of its products—the same goes for Google, for Amazon, and for every other large technology company. Companies that adopt microservice architecture will never be an exception to this rule.

Microservice architecture is comprised of a large number of small, isolated, independent microservices. The Inverse Conway's Law demands that the organizational structure of any company using microservice architecture will be made up of a large number of very small, isolated, and independent teams. The team structures that spring from this inevitably lead to siloing and sprawl, problems that are made worse every time the microservice ecosystem becomes more sophisticated, more complex, more concurrent, and more efficient.

Inverse Conway's Law also means that developers will be, in some ways, just like microservices: they will be able to do one thing, and (hopefully) do that one thing very well, but they will be isolated (in responsibility, in domain knowledge, and experience) from the rest of the ecosystem. When considered together, all of the developers *collectively* working within a microservice ecosystem will know everything there is to know about it, but individually they will be extremely specialized, knowing only the pieces of the ecosystem they are responsible for.

This poses an unavoidable organizational problem: even though microservices must be developed in isolation (leading to isolated, siloed teams), they don't live in isolation and must interact with one another seamlessly if the overall product is to function at all. This requires that these isolated, independently functioning teams work together closely and often—something that is difficult to accomplish, given that most team's goals and projects (codified in their team's objectives and key results, or OKRs) are specific to a particular microservice they are working on.

There is also a large communication gap between microservice teams and infrastructure teams that needs to be closed. Application platform teams, for example, need to build platform services and tools that all of the microservice teams will use, but gaining the requirements and needs from hundreds of microservice teams before building one small project can take months (even years). Getting developers and infrastructure teams to work together is not an easy task.

There's a related problem that arises thanks to Inverse Conway's Law, one that is only rarely found in companies with monolithic architecture: the difficulty of running an operations organization. With a monolith, an operations organization can easily be staffed and on call for the application, but this is very difficult to achieve with microservice architecture because it would require every single microservice to be staffed by both a development team *and* an operational team. Consequently, microservice development teams need to be responsible for the operational duties and tasks associated with their microservice. There is no separate ops org to take over the on call, no separate ops org responsible for monitoring: developers will need to be on call for their services.

Technical Sprawl

The second trade-off, *technical sprawl*, is related to the first. While Conway's Law and its inverse predict organizational sprawl and siloing for microservices, a second type of sprawl (related to technologies, tools, and the like) is also unavoidable in microservice architecture. There are many different ways in which technical sprawl can manifest. We'll cover a few of the most common ways here.

It's easy to see why microservice architecture leads to technical sprawl if we consider a large microservice ecosystem, one containing 1,000 microservices. Suppose each of these microservices is staffed by a development team of six developers, and each developer uses their own set of favorite tools, favorite libraries, and works in their own favorite languages. Each of these development teams has their own way of deploying, their own specified metrics to monitor and alert on, their own external libraries and internal dependencies they use, custom scripts to run on production machines, and so on.

If you have a thousand of these teams, this means that within one system there are a thousand ways to do one thing. There will be a thousand ways to deploy, a thousand libraries to maintain, a thousand different ways of alerting and monitoring and testing and handling outages. The only way to cut down on technical sprawl is through standardization at every level of the microservice ecosystem.

There's another kind of technical sprawl associated with language choice. Microservices infamously come with the promise of greater developer freedom, freedom to choose whichever languages and libraries one wants. This is possible in principle, and can be true in practice, but as a microservice ecosystem grows it often becomes impractical, costly, and dangerous. To see why this can become a problem, consider the following scenario. Suppose we have a microservice ecosystem containing 200 services, and imagine that some of these microservices are written in Python, others in JavaScript, some in Haskell, a few in Go, and a couple more in Ruby, Java, and C++. For each internal tool, for each system and service within every layer of the ecosystem, libraries will have to be written for each one of these languages.

Take a moment to contemplate the sheer amount of maintenance and development that will have to be done in order for each language to receive the support it requires: it's extraordinary, and very few engineering organizations could afford to dedicate the engineering resources necessary to make it happen. It's more realistic to choose a small number of supported languages and ensure that all libraries and tools are compatible with and exist for these languages than to attempt to support a large number of languages.

The last type of technical sprawl we will cover here is technical debt, which usually refers to work that needs to be done because something was implemented in a way that got the job done quickly, but not in the best or most optimal way. Given that microservice development teams can churn out new features at a fast pace, technical debt often builds up quietly in the background. When outages happen, when things break, any work that comes out of an incident review will only rarely be the best overall solution: as far as microservice development teams are concerned, whatever fixes (or fixed) the problem quickly and in the moment was good enough, and any better solutions are pawned off to the future.

More Ways to Fail

Microservices are large, complex, distributed systems with many small, independent pieces that are constantly changing. The reality of working with complex systems of this sort is that individual components will fail, they will fail often, and they will fail in ways that nobody could have predicted. This is where the third trade-off comes into play: microservice architecture introduces more ways your system can fail.

There are ways to prepare for failure, to mitigate failures when they occur, and to test the limits and boundaries of both the individual components and the overall ecosystem, which I cover in Chapter 5, *Fault Tolerance and Catastrophe-Preparedness*. However, it is important to understand that no matter how many resiliency tests you run, no matter how many failures and catastrophe scenarios you've scoped out, you cannot escape the fact that the system *will* fail. You can only do your best to prepare for when it does.

Competition for Resources

Just like any other ecosystem in the natural world, competition for resources in the microservice ecosystem is fierce. Each engineering organization has finite resources: it has finite engineering resources (teams, developers) and finite hardware and infrastructure resources (physical machines, cloud hardware, database storage, etc.), and each resource costs the company a great deal of money.

When your microservice ecosystem has a large number of microservices and a large and sophisticated application platform, competition between teams for hardware and infrastructure resources is inevitable: every service, every tool will be presented as equally important, its scaling needs presented as being of the highest priority.

Likewise, when application platform teams are asking for specifications and needs from microservice teams so that they can design their systems and tools appropriately, every microservice development team will argue that their needs are the most important and will be disappointed (and potentially very frustrated) if they are not included. This kind of competition for engineering resources can lead to resentment between teams.

The last kind of competition for resources is perhaps the most obvious one: the competition between managers, between teams, and between different engineering departments/organization for engineering headcount. Even with the increase in computer science graduates and the rise of developer bootcamps, truly great developers are difficult to find, and represent one of the most irreplaceable and scarce resources. When there are hundreds or thousands of teams that could use an extra engineer or two, every single team will insist that their team needs an extra engineer more than any of the other teams.

There is no way to avoid competition for resources, though there are ways to mitigate competition somewhat. The most effective seems to be organizing or categorizing teams in terms of their importance and criticality to the overall business, and then giving teams access to resources based on their priority or importance. There are downsides to this, because it tends to result in poorly staffed development tools teams, and in projects whose importance lies in shaping the future (such as adopting new infrastructure technologies) being abandoned.

CHAPTER 2

Production-Readiness

While the adoption of microservice architecture brings considerable freedom to developers, ensuring availability across the microservice ecosystem requires holding individual microservices to high architectural, operational, and organizational standards. This chapter covers the challenges of microservice standardization, introduces availability as the goal of standardization, presents the eight production-readiness standards, and proposes strategies for implementing production-readiness standardization across an engineering organization.

The Challenges of Microservice Standardization

The architecture of a monolithic application is usually determined at the beginning of the application's lifecycle. For many applications, the architecture is determined at the time a company begins. As the business grows, and the application scales, developers who are adding new features often find themselves constrained and limited by the choices made when the application was first designed. They are constrained by choice of language, by the libraries they are able to use, by the development tools they can work with, and by the need for extensive regression testing to ensure that every new feature they add does not disturb or compromise the entirety of the application. Any refactoring that happens to the standalone, monolithic application is still essentially constrained by initial architectural decisions: initial conditions exclusively determine the future of the application.

The adoption of microservice architecture brings a considerable amount of freedom to developers. They are no longer tied to the architectural decisions of the past, they can architect their service however they wish, and they have free reign in decisions of language, of database, of development tools, and the like. The message accompanying the adoption of microservice architecture is usually understood and heard by developers as follows: build an application that does one thing—one thing only—and does that one thing *extraordinarily well*; do whatever you need to do, build it however you want—just make sure it gets the job done.

While this romantic idealization of microservice development is true in principle, not all microservices are created equal—nor should they be. Each microservice is part of a microservice ecosystem, and complex dependency chains are a necessary inevitability. When you have 100, 1,000, or even 10,000 microservices, each of them will be playing a small role in a very large system. The services must interact seamlessly with one another, and—most importantly—no service or set of services should compromise the integrity of the overall system or product that they comprise. If the overall system or product is to be any good, it must be held to certain standards, and consequently, each of its parts must abide by these standards as well.

It's relatively simple to determine standards and give requirements to a microservice team if we focus on the needs of that specific team and the role their service is to play. We can say, "your microservice must do x, y, and z, and to do x, y, and z well, you need to make sure you meet this set S of requirements," giving each team a set of requirements that is relevant to their service, and to their service alone. Unfortunately, this approach simply isn't scalable and neglects to recognize the important fact that a microservice is but a very small piece of an absurdly large and distributed puzzle. We must define standards and requirements for our microservices, and they must be general enough to apply to every single microservice yet specific enough to be quantifiable and produce measurable results. This is where the concept of *production-readiness* comes in.

Availability: The Goal of Standardization

Within microservice ecosystems, service-level agreements (SLAs) regarding the availability of a service are the most commonly used methods of measuring a service's success: if a service is highly available (that is, has very little downtime), then we can say with reasonable confidence (and a few caveats) that the service is doing its job.

Calculating and measuring availability is easy. You need to calculate only three measurable quantities: *uptime* (the length of time that the microservice worked correctly), *downtime* (the length of time that the microservice was *not* working correctly), and the total time a service was operational (the sum of uptime and downtime). Availability is then the uptime divided by the total time a service was operational (uptime + downtime).

As useful as it is, availability is not in itself a principle of microservice standardization, but the goal. It can't be a principle of standardization because it gives no guidance as to how to architect, build, or run the microservice: telling developers to make their microservice more available without telling them how (or *why*) to do so is useless. Availability alone comes with no concrete, applicable steps, but as we will see in the following sections, there are concrete, applicable steps that can be taken toward reaching the goal of building an available microservice.

Calculating Availability

Availability is measured in so-called nines notation, which corresponds to the percentage of time that a service is available. For example, a service that is available 99% of the time is said to have "two-nines availability."

This notation is useful because it gives us a specific amount of downtime that a service is allowed to have. If your service is required to have four-nines availability, then it is allowed 52.56 minutes of downtime per year, which is 4.38 minutes of downtime per month, 1.01 minutes of downtime per week, and 8.66 seconds of downtime per day.

Here are the availability and downtime calculations for 99% availability to 99.999% availability:

99% availability: (two-nines)

- 3.65 days/year (of allowed downtime)
- 7.20 hours/month
- 1.68 hours/week
- 14.4 minutes/day

99.9% availability (three-nines):

- 8.76 hours/year
- 43.8 minutes/month
- 10.1 minutes/week
- 1.44 minutes/day

99.99% availability (four-nines):

- 52.56 minutes/year
- 4.38 minutes/month
- 1.01 minutes/week
- 8.66 seconds/day

99.999% availability (five-nines):

- 5.26 minutes/year
- 25.9 seconds/month
- 6.05 seconds/week
- 864.3 milliseconds/day

Production-Readiness Standards

The basic idea behind production-readiness is this: a production-ready application or service is one that can be trusted to serve production traffic. When we refer to an application or microservice as "production-ready," we confer a great deal of trust upon it: we trust it to behave reasonably, we trust it to perform reliably, we trust it to get the job done and to do its job well with very little downtime. Production-readiness is the key to microservice standardization, the key to achieving availability across the microservice ecosystem.

However, the idea of production-readiness as stated isn't useful enough on its own to serve as the exhaustive definition we need, and without further explication, the concept isn't very helpful. We need to know exactly what requirements every service must meet in order to be deemed production-ready and to be trusted to serve production traffic in a reliable, appropriate way—a trust that can't be given freely, but has to be earned. The requirements must themselves be principles that are true for every microservice, for every application, and for every distributed system: standardization without principle is meaningless.

It turns out that there is a set of eight principles that, when adopted together, fits these criteria. Each of these principles is quantifiable, gives rise to a set of actionable requirements, and produces measurable results. They are: *stability, reliability, scalability, fault tolerance, catastrophe-preparedness, performance, monitoring,* and *documentation.* The driving force behind each of these principles is that, together, they contribute to and drive the *availability* of a microservice.

Availability is, in some ways, an emergent property of a production-ready microservice. It emerges from building a scalable, reliable, fault-tolerant, performant, monitored, documented, and catastrophe-prepared microservice. Any one of these principles individually is not enough to ensure availability, but together they are: building a microservice with these principles as the driving architectural and operational requirements guarantees a highly available system that can be trusted with production traffic.

Stability

With the introduction of microservice architecture, developers are given freedom to develop and deploy at a very high velocity. New features can be added and deployed each day, bugs can be quickly fixed, any old technologies swapped out for the newest ones, and outdated microservices can be rewritten and the old versions deprecated and decommissioned. With this increased velocity comes increased instability, and in microservice ecosystems the majority of outages can usually be traced back to a bad deployment that contained buggy code or other serious errors. To ensure availability, we need to carefully guard against this instability that stems from increased developer velocity and the constant evolution of the microservice ecosystem.

Stability allows us to reach availability by giving us ways to responsibly handle changes to microservices. A stable microservice is one in which development, deployment, the addition of new technologies, and the decommissioning and deprecation of microservices do not give rise to instability within and across the larger microservice ecosystem. We can determine stability requirements for each microservice to mitigate the negative side effects that may accompany each change.

To mitigate any problems that may arise from the development cycle, stable development procedures can be put into place. To counteract any instability introduced by deployment, we can ensure our microservices are deployed carefully with proper staging, canary (a small pool of 2%–5% of production hosts), and production rollouts. To prevent the introduction of new technologies and the deprecation and decommissioning of old microservices from compromising the availability of other services, we can enforce stable introduction and deprecation procedures.

Stability Requirements

The requirements of building a stable microservice are:

- A stable development cycle
- A stable deployment process
- Stable introduction and deprecation procedures

The details of stability requirements are covered in *Chapter 3, Stability and Reliability.*

Reliability

Stability alone isn't enough to ensure a microservice's availability: the service must also be *reliable.* A reliable microservice is one that can be trusted by its clients, by its dependencies, and by the microservice ecosystem as a whole. A reliable microservice is one that has truly earned the trust that is essential and required in order for it to serve production traffic.

While stability is related to mitigating the negative side effects accompanying change, and reliability is related to trust, the two are inextricably linked. Each stability requirement also carries a reliability requirement alongside it: for example, developers should not only seek to have stable deployment processes, they should also ensure that each deployment is reliable from the point of view of one of their clients or dependencies.

The trust that reliability secures can be broken into several requirements, the same way we determined requirements for stability. For example, we can make our deployment processes reliable by making sure that our integration tests are comprehensive and our staging and canary deployment phases are successful so that every change introduced into production can be trusted not to contain any errors that might compromise its clients and dependencies.

By building reliability into our microservices, we can protect their availability. We can cache data so that it will be readily available to client services, helping them protect their SLAs by making our own services highly available. To protect our own SLA from any problems with the availability of our dependencies, we can implement defensive caching.

The last reliability requirement is related to routing and discovery. Availability requires that the communication and routing between different services be reliable: health checks should be accurate, requests and responses should reach their destinations, and errors should be handled carefully and appropriately.

Reliability Requirements

The requirements of building a reliable microservice are:

- A reliable deployment process
- Planning, mitigating, and protecting against the failures of dependencies
- Reliable routing and discovery

The details of production-ready reliability requirements are covered in *Chapter 3, Stability and Reliability*.

Scalability

Microservice traffic is rarely static or constant, and one of the hallmarks of a successful microservice (and of a successful microservice ecosystem) is a steady increase in traffic. Microservices need to be built in preparation for this growth, they need to

---

accommodate it easily, and they need to be able to actively scale with it. A microservice that can't scale with growth experiences increased latency, poor availability, and in extreme cases, a drastic increase in incidents and outages. *Scalability* is essential for availability, making it our third production-readiness standard.

A scalable microservice is one that can handle a large number of tasks or requests at the same time. To ensure a microservice is scalable, we need to know both (1) its qualitative growth scale (e.g., whether it scales with page views or customer orders) and (2) its quantitative growth scale (e.g., how many requests per second it can handle). Once we know the growth scale, we can plan for future capacity needs and identify resource bottlenecks and requirements.

The way a microservice handles traffic should also be scalable. It should be prepared for bursts of traffic, handle them carefully, and prevent them from taking down the service entirely. It's easier said than done, but without scalable traffic handling, developers can (and will) find themselves looking at a broken microservice ecosystem.

Additional complexity is introduced by the rest of the microservice ecosystem. The inevitable additional traffic and growth from a service's clients have to be prepared for. Likewise, any dependencies of the service should be alerted when increases in traffic are expected. Cross-team communication and collaboration are essential for scalability: regularly communicating with clients and dependencies about a service's scalability requirements, status, and any bottlenecks ensures that any services relying on each other are prepared for growth and for potential pitfalls.

Last but not least, the way a microservice stores and handles data needs to be scalable as well. Building a scalable storage solution goes a long way toward ensuring the availability of a microservice, and is one of the most essential components of a truly production-ready system.

Scalability Requirements

The requirements of building a scalable microservice are:

- Well-defined quantitative and qualitative growth scales
- Identification of resource bottlenecks and requirements
- Careful, accurate capacity planning
- Scalable handling of traffic
- The scaling of dependencies
- Scalable data storage

The details of production-ready scalability requirements are covered in *Chapter 4, Scalability and Performance.*

Fault Tolerance and Catastrophe-Preparedness

Even the simplest of microservices is a fairly complex system. As we know quite well, complex systems fail, they fail often, and any potential failure scenario can and will happen at some point in the microservice's lifetime. Microservices don't live in isolation, but within dependency chains as part of a larger, incredibly complex microservice ecosystem. The complexity scales linearly with the number of microservice in the overall ecosystem, and ensuring the availability of not only an individual microservice, but the ecosystem as a whole, requires that we impose yet another production-readiness standard onto each microservice. Every microservice within the ecosystem must be *fault tolerant* and *prepared for any catastrophe.*

A fault-tolerant, catastrophe-prepared microservice is one that can withstand both internal and external failures. Internal failures are those that the microservice brings on itself: for example, code bugs that aren't caught by proper testing lead to bad deploys, causing outages that affect the entire ecosystem. External catastrophes, such as datacenter outages and/or poor configuration management across the ecosystem, lead to outages that affect the availability of every microservice and the entire organization.

Failure scenarios and potential catastrophes can be quite adequately (though not exhaustively) prepared for. Identifying failure and catastrophe scenarios is the first requirement of building a fault-tolerant, production-ready microservice. Once these scenarios have been identified, the hard work of strategizing and planning for when they will occur begins. This has to happen at every level of the microservice ecosystem, and any shared strategies should be communicated across the organization so that mitigation is standardized and predictable.

Standardization of failure mitigation and resolution at the organizational level means that incidents and outages of individual microservices, infrastructure components, or the ecosystem as a whole need to be wrapped into carefully executed, easily understandable procedures. Incident response procedures need to be handled in a coordinated, planned, and thoroughly communicated manner. If incidents and outages are handled in this way, and the structure of incident response is well defined, organizations can avoid lengthy downtimes and protect the availability of the microservices. If every developer knows exactly what they are supposed to do in an outage, knows how to mitigate and resolve problems quickly and appropriately, and knows how to escalate if an issue is beyond their capabilities or control, then the time to mitigation and time to resolution drop drastically.

Making failures and catastrophes predictable means going one step further after identifying failure and catastrophe scenarios and planning for them. It means forcing the microservices, the infrastructure, and the ecosystem to fail in any and all known ways to test the availability of the entire system. This is accomplished through various types of resiliency testing. Code testing (including unit tests, regression tests, and integration tests) is the first step in testing for resiliency. The second step is load testing, where microservices and infrastructure components are tested for their ability to handle drastic changes in traffic. The last, most intense, and most relevant type of resiliency testing is chaos testing, in which failure scenarios are run (both scheduled and randomly) on production services to ensure that microservices and infrastructure components are truly prepared for all known failure scenarios.

Fault Tolerance and Catastrophe-Preparedness Requirements

The requirements of building a fault-tolerant microservice that is prepared for any catastrophe are:

- Potential catastrophes and failure scenarios are identified and planned for.
- Single points of failure are identified and resolved.
- Failure detection and remediation strategies are in place.
- It is tested for resiliency through code testing, load testing, and chaos testing.
- Traffic is managed carefully in preparation for failure.
- Incidents and outages are handled appropriately and productively.

The details of production-ready fault tolerance and catastrophe-preparedness requirements are covered in *Chapter 5, Fault Tolerance and Catastrophe-Preparedness.*

Performance

In the context of the microservice ecosystem, scalability (which we covered in brief detail earlier), is related to how many requests a microservice can handle. Our next production-readiness principle—*performance*—refers to how well the microservice handles those requests. A performant microservice is one that handles requests quickly, processes tasks efficiently, and properly utilizes resources (such as hardware and other infrastructure components).

A microservice that makes a large number of expensive network calls, for example, is not performant. Neither is a microservice that processes and handles tasks synchronously in cases when asynchronous (nonblocking) task processing would increase the performance and availability of the service. Identifying and architecting away these performance problems is a strict production-readiness requirement.

Similarly, dedicating a large number of resources (like CPU) to a microservice that doesn't utilize it is inefficient. Inefficiency reduces performance: if it's not clear at the microservice level in every case, it's painful and costly at the ecosystem level. Underutilized hardware resources affects the bottom line, and hardware is not cheap. There's a fine line between underutilization and proper capacity planning, and so the two must be planned and understood together in order for the availability of the microservice to not be compromised and the cost of underutilization reasonable.

Performance Requirements

The requirements of building a performant microservice are:

- Appropriate service-level agreements (SLAs) for availability
- Proper task handling and processing
- Efficient utilization of resources

The details of production-ready performance requirements are covered in *Chapter 4, Scalability and Performance*.

Monitoring

Another principle necessary for guaranteeing microservice availability is proper microservice *monitoring*. Good monitoring has three components: proper logging of all important and relevant information; useful graphical displays (dashboards) that are easily understood by any developer in the company and that accurately reflect the health of the services; and alerting on key metrics that is effective and actionable.

Logging belongs and begins in the codebase of each microservice. Determining precisely what information to log will differ for each service, but the goal of logging is quite simple: when faced with a bug—even one from many deployments in the past— you want and need your logging to be such that you can determine from the logs exactly what went wrong and where things fell apart. In microservice ecosystems, the versioning of microservices is discouraged, so you won't have a precise version to refer to in which to find any bugs or problems. Code is revised frequently, deployments happen multiple times per week, features are added constantly, and dependencies are ever-changing, but logs will stay the same, preserving the information needed to pinpoint any problems. Just make sure your logs contain the information necessary to determine possible problems.

All key metrics (such as hardware utilization, database connections, responses and average response times, and the status of API endpoints) should be graphically displayed in real time on an easily accessible dashboard. Dashboards are an important component of building a well-monitored, production-ready microservice: they make it easy to determine the health of a microservice with one glance and enable developers to detect strange patterns and anomalies that may not be extreme enough to trigger alerting thresholds. When used wisely, dashboards allow developers to determine whether or not a microservice is working correctly simply by looking at the dashboard, but developers should never need to watch the dashboard in order to detect incidents and outages, and rollbacks to stable previous builds should be fully automated.

The actual detection of failures is accomplished through alerting. All key metrics must be alerted on, including (at the very least) CPU and RAM utilization, number of file descriptors, number of database connections, the SLA of the service, requests and responses, the status of API endpoints, errors and exceptions, the health of the service's dependencies, information about any database(s), and the number of tasks being processed (if applicable).

Normal, warning, and critical thresholds need to be set for each of these key metrics, and any deviation from the norm (i.e., hitting the warning or critical thresholds) should trigger an alert to the developers who are on call for the service. Thresholds should be signal-providing: high enough to avoid noise, but low enough to catch any and all real problems.

Alerts need to be useful and actionable. A nonactionable alert is not a useful alert, and a waste of engineering hours. Every actionable alert—that is, *every* alert—should be accompanied by a runbook. For example, if an alert is triggered on a high number of exceptions of a certain type, then there needs to be a runbook containing mitigation strategies that any on-call developer can refer to while attempting to resolve the problem.

Monitoring Requirements

The requirements of building a properly monitored microservice are:

- Proper logging and tracing throughout the stack
- Well-designed dashboards that are easy to understand and accurately reflect the health of the service
- Effective, actionable alerting accompanied by runbooks
- Implementing and maintaining an on-call rotation

The details of production-ready monitoring requirements are covered in *Chapter 6, Monitoring*.

Documentation

Microservice architecture carries the potential for increased technical debt—it's one of the key trade-offs that come with adopting microservices. As a rule, technical debt tends to increase *with* developer velocity: the more quickly a service can be iterated on, changed, and deployed, the more frequently shortcuts and patches will be put into place. Organizational clarity and structure around the *documentation* and *under-*

standing of a microservice cut through this technical debt and shave off a lot of the confusion, lack of awareness, and lack of architectural comprehension that tend to accompany it.

Reducing technical debt isn't the only reason to make good documentation a production-readiness principle: doing so would make it somewhat of an afterthought (an important afterthought, but an afterthought nonetheless). No, just like each of the other production-readiness standards, documentation and its counterpart (understanding) directly and measurably influence the availability of a microservice.

To see why this is true, we can think about how teams of developers work together and share their knowledge and understanding of a microservice. You can do this yourself by sitting one of your development teams in a room, in front of a whiteboard, and asking them to sketch the architecture and all important details of the service. I promise you will be surprised by the result of this exercise, and you will most likely find that knowledge and understanding of the service is not cohesive or coherent across the group. One developer will know one thing about the application that nobody else does, while a second developer will have such a different understanding of the microservice that you will wonder if they are even contributing to the same codebase. When it's time for code changes to be reviewed, technologies to be swapped, or features to be added, the lack of alignment of knowledge and understanding will lead to the design and/or evolution of microservices that are not production-ready, containing serious flaws that undermine the service's ability to reliably serve production traffic.

This confusion and the problems that it creates can be successfully and rather easily avoided by requiring that every microservice follow a very strictly standardized set of documentation requirements. Documentation needs to contain all the essential knowledge (facts) about a microservice, including an architecture diagram, an onboarding and development guide, details about the request flow and any API endpoints, and an on-call runbook for each of the service's alerts.

Understanding of a microservice can be accomplished in several ways. The first is by doing the exercise I just mentioned: stick the development team in a conference room, and ask them to whiteboard the architecture of the service. Thanks to our old friend, the ever-present increased developer velocity, microservices change radically at different times throughout their lifecycle. By making these architecture reviews part of each team's process and scheduling them regularly, you can guarantee that knowledge and understanding about any changes in the microservice will be disseminated to the entire team.

To cover the second aspect of microservice understanding, we need to jump up by one level of abstraction and consider the production-readiness standards themselves. A great deal of microservice understanding is captured by determining whether a microservice is production-ready and where it stands with regard to the production-readiness standards and their individual requirements. This can be accomplished in a myriad of ways, one of which is running audits of whether a microservice meets the requirements, and then creating a roadmap for the service detailing how to bring it to a production-ready state. Checking the requirements can also be automated across the organization. We'll dive into other aspects of this in more detail in the next section on the implementation of production-readiness standards in an organization that has adopted microservice architecture.

Documentation Requirements

The requirements of building a well-documented microservice are:

- Thorough, updated, and centralized documentation containing all of the relevant and essential information about the microservice
- Organizational understanding at the developer, team, and ecosystem levels

The details of production-ready documentation requirements are covered in *Chapter 7, Documentation and Understanding.*

Implementing Production-Readiness

We now have a set of standards that apply to every microservice in any microservice ecosystem, each with its own set of specific requirements. Any microservice that satisfies these requirements can be trusted to serve production traffic and guarantee a high level of availability.

Now that we have the production-readiness standards, the question that remains is *how* we can implement them in a specialized, real-world microservice ecosystem. Going from principle to practice and applying theory to real-world applications always presents us with some significant level of difficulty. However, the power of these production-readiness standards and the requirements they impose lies in their remarkable applicability and strict granularity: they are both general enough to apply to any ecosystem, yet specific enough to provide concrete strategies for implementation.

Standardization requires buy-in from all levels of the organization, and must be adopted and driven both from the top-down and from the bottom-up. At the executive and leadership (managerial and technical) levels, these principles need to be driven and supported as architectural requirements for the engineering organization. On the ground floor, within individual development teams, standardization needs to be embraced and implemented. Importantly, standardization needs to be seen and communicated not as a hindrance or gate to development and deployment, but as a guide for production-ready development and deployment.

Many developers may resist standardization. After all, they may argue, isn't the point of adopting microservice architecture to provide greater developer velocity, freedom, and productivity? The answer to these sorts of objections is not to deny that the adoption of microservice architecture brings freedom and velocity to development teams, but to agree and point out that that is *exactly* why production-readiness standards need to be in place. Developer velocity and productivity grind to a halt whenever an outage brings a service down, whenever a bad deploy compromises the availability of a microservice's clients and dependencies, whenever a failure that *could have been avoided with proper resiliency testing* brings the entire microservice ecosystem down. If we've learned anything in the past 50 years about software development, we've learned that standardization brings freedom and reduces entropy. As Brooks says in *The Mythical Man-Month*, perhaps the greatest collection of essays on the practice of software engineering, "form is liberating."

Once the engineering organization has adopted and agreed to follow production-readiness standards, the next step is to evaluate and elaborate on each standard's requirements. The requirements presented here and detailed throughout this book are very general and need the addition of context and organization-specific details and implementation strategies. What needs to be done is to work through each production-readiness standard and its requirements and to figure out how each requirement can be implemented in the engineering organization. For example, if the organization's microservice ecosystem has a self-service deployment tool, then implementing a stable and reliable deployment process needs to be communicated in terms of the internal deployment tool and how it works. Rebuilding internal tools and/or adding features to them may also come out of this exercise.

The actual implementation of the requirements and determining whether or not a given microservice meets them can be done by the developers themselves, by team leads, by management, or by operations (systems, DevOps, or site reliability) engineers. At both Uber and the several other companies I know that have adopted production-readiness standardization, the implementation and enforcement of the production-readiness standards is driven by the site reliability engineering (SRE) organizations. Typically, SREs are responsible for the availability of the services, and so driving these standards across the microservice ecosystem fits in quite well with existing responsibilities. That isn't to say that the developers or development teams have no responsibility for ensuring their services are production-ready; rather, SREs inform, drive, and enforce production-readiness within the microservice ecosystem, and the responsibility of implementation falls on both the SREs embedded within development teams and on the developers themselves.

Building and maintaining a production-ready microservice ecosystem is not an easy challenge to undertake, but the rewards are great, and the impact can be seen so clearly in the increased availability of each microservice. Implementing production-readiness standards and their requirements provides measurable results, and means that development teams can work knowing that the services they depend on are trust-worthy, that they are stable, reliable, fault tolerant, performant, monitored, docu-mented, and prepared for any catastrophe.

CHAPTER 3

Stability and Reliability

A production-ready microservice is stable and reliable. Both individual microservices and the overall microservice ecosystem are constantly changing and evolving, and any efforts made to increase the stability and reliability of a microservice go a long way toward ensuring the health and availability of the overall ecosystem. In this chapter, different ways to build and run a stable and reliable microservice are explored, including standardizing the development process, building comprehensive deployment pipelines, understanding dependencies and protecting against their failures, building stable and reliable routing and discovery, and establishing appropriate deprecation and decommissioning procedures for old or outdated microservices and/or their endpoints.

Principles of Building Stable and Reliable Microservices

Microservice architecture lends itself to fast-paced development. The freedom offered by microservices means that the ecosystem will be in a state of continuous change, never static, always evolving. Features will be added every day, new builds will be deployed multiple times per day, and old technologies will be swapped for newer and better ones at an astounding pace. This freedom and flexibility gives rise to real, tangible innovation, but comes at a great cost.

Innovation, increased developer velocity and productivity, rapid technological advancement, and the ever-changing microservice ecosystem can all very quickly be brought to a screeching halt if any piece of the microservice ecosystem becomes unstable or unreliable. In some cases, all it takes to bring the entire business down is deploying a broken build or a build containing a bug to one business-critical microservice.

A *stable* microservice is one for which development, deployment, the adoption of new technologies, and the decommissioning or deprecation of other services do not give rise to instability across the larger microservice ecosystem. This requires putting measures into place to protect against the negative consequences that may be introduced by these types of changes. A *reliable* microservice is one that can be trusted by other microservices and by the overall ecosystem. Stability goes hand in hand with reliability because each stability requirement carries with it a reliability requirement (and vice versa): for example, stable deployment processes are accompanied by a requirement that each new deployment does not compromise the reliability of the microservice from the point of view of one of their clients or dependencies.

There are several things that can be done to ensure that a microservice is stable and reliable. A standardized *development cycle* can be implemented to protect against poor development practices. The *deployment* process can be designed so that changes to the code are forced to pass through multiple stages before being rolled out to all production servers. *Dependency* failures can be protected against. Health checks, proper routing, and circuit breaking can be built into the *routing and discovery* channels to handle anomalous traffic patterns. Finally, microservices and their endpoints can be *deprecated* and/or *decommissioned* without causing any failures for other microservices.

A Production-Ready Service Is Stable and Reliable

- It has a standardized development cycle.
- Its code is thoroughly tested through lint, unit, integration, and end-to-end testing.
- Its test, packaging, build, and release process is completely automated.
- It has a standardized deployment pipeline, containing staging, canary, and production phases.
- Its clients are known.
- Its dependencies are known, and there are backups, alternatives, fallbacks, and caching in place in case of failures.
- It has stable and reliable routing and discovery in place.

The Development Cycle

The stability and reliability of a microservice begins with the individual developer who is contributing code to the service. The majority of outages and microservice failures are caused by bugs introduced into the code that were not caught in the development phase, in any of the tests, or at any step in the deployment process. Mitigating and resolving these outages and failures usually entails nothing more than rolling back to the latest stable build, reverting whatever commit contained the bug, and re-deploying a new (bug-less) version of the code.

The True Cost of Unstable and Unreliable Development

A microservice ecosystem is not the Wild West. Every outage, every incident, and every bug can and will cost the company thousands (if not millions) of dollars in engineering hours and lost revenue. Safeguards need to be in place during the development cycle (and, as we will see, in the deployment pipeline) to catch every bug before it hits production.

A stable and reliable development cycle has several steps (Figure 3-1).

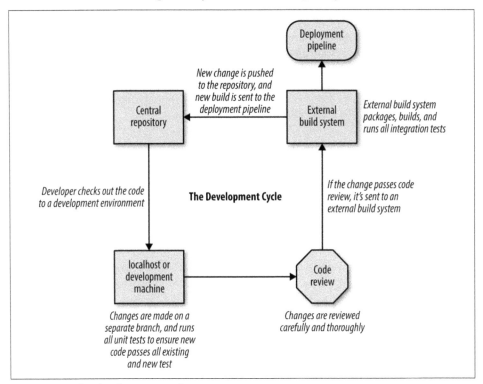

Figure 3-1. The development cycle

First, the developer makes a change to the code. This will usually begin with checking a copy of the code out from a central repository (usually using git or svn), creating an individual branch where they will make changes, adding their changes to their branch, and running any unit and integration tests. This stage of development can happen anywhere: locally on a developer's laptop or on a server in a development environment. A reliable development environment—one that accurately mirrors the production world—is key, especially if testing the service in question requires making requests to other microservices or reading or writing data to a database.

Once the code has been committed to the central repository, the second step consists in having the change(s) reviewed carefully and thoroughly by other engineers on the team. If all reviewers have approved the change(s), and all lint, unit, and integration tests have passed on a new build, the change can be merged into the repository (see Chapter 5, *Fault Tolerance and Catastrophe-Preparedness*, for more on lint, unit, and integration tests). Then, and only then, can the new change be introduced into the deployment pipeline.

Test Before Code Review

One way to ensure that all bugs are caught before they hit production is to run all lint, unit, integration, and end-to-end tests *before* the code review phase. This can be accomplished by having developers work on a separate branch, kicking off all tests on that branch as soon as the developer submits it for code review, and then only allowing it to reach code review (or only allowing it to be built) *after* it successfully passes all tests.

As mentioned in the section on layer 4 of the microservice ecosystem in Chapter 1, *Microservices*, a lot happens in between the development cycle and the deployment pipeline. The new release needs to be packaged, built, and thoroughly tested before reaching the first stage of the deployment pipeline.

The Deployment Pipeline

There is a great deal of room for human error in microservice ecosystems, especially where deployment practices are concerned, and (as I mentioned earlier) the majority of outages in large-scale production systems are caused by bad deployments. Consider the organizational sprawl that accompanies the adoption of microservice architecture and what it entails for the deployment process: you have, at the very least, dozens (if not hundreds or thousands) of independent, isolated teams who are deploying changes to their microservices on their own schedules, and often without cross-team coordination between clients and dependencies. If something goes wrong, if a bug is introduced into production, or if a service is temporarily unavailable during deployment, then the entire ecosystem can be negatively affected. To ensure that things go wrong with less frequency, and that any failures can be caught before being rolled out to all production servers, introducing a standardized *deployment pipeline* across the engineering organization can help ensure stability and reliability across the ecosystem.

I refer to the deployment process here as a "pipeline" because the most trustworthy deployments are those that have been required to pass a set of tests before reaching production servers. We can fit three separate stages or phases into this pipeline (Figure 3-2): first, we can test a new release in a *staging* environment; second, if it passes the staging phase, we can deploy it to a small *canary* environment, where it will serve 5%–10% of production traffic; and third, if it passes the canary phase, we can slowly roll it out to *production* servers until it has been deployed to every host.

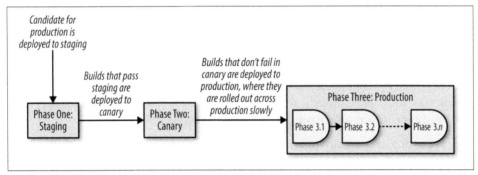

Figure 3-2. Stages of a stable and reliable deployment pipeline

Staging

Any new release can first be deployed to a *staging* environment. A staging environment should be an exact copy of the production environment: it is a reflection of the state of the real world, but without real traffic. Staging environments usually aren't running at the same scale as production (i.e., they typically aren't run with the same number of hosts as production, a phenomenon also known as *host parity*), because running what would amount to two separate ecosystems can present a large hardware cost to the company. However, some engineering organizations may determine that the only way to accurately copy the production environment in a stable and reliable way is to build an identical staging environment with host parity.

For most engineering organizations, determining the hardware capacity and scale of the staging environment as a percentage of production is usually accurate enough. The necessary staging capacity can be determined by the method we will use to test the microservice within the staging phase. To test in the staging environment, we have several options: we can run mock (or recorded) traffic through the microservice; we can test it manually by hitting its endpoints and evaluating its responses; we can run automated unit, integration, and other specialized tests; or we can test each new release with any combination of these methods.

Treat Staging and Production as Separate Deployments of the Same Service

You may be tempted to run staging and production as separate services and store them in separate repositories. This *can* be done successfully, but it requires that changes be synchronized across both services and repositories, including configuration changes (which are often forgotten about). It's much easier to treat staging and production as separate "deployments" or "phases" of the same microservice.

Even though staging environments *are* testing environments, they differ from both the development phase and the development environment in that a release that has been deployed to staging is a release that is a *candidate for production*. A candidate for production must have already successfully passed lint tests, unit tests, integration tests, and code review before being deployed to a staging environment.

Deploying to a staging environment should be treated by developers with the same seriousness and caution as deploying to production. If a release is successfully deployed to staging, it can be automatically deployed to canaries, which *will* be running production traffic.

Setting up staging environments in a microservice ecosystem can be difficult, due to the complexities introduced by dependencies. If your microservice depends on nine other microservices, then it relies on those dependencies to give accurate responses when requests are sent and reads or writes to the relevant database(s) are made. As a consequence of these complexities, the success of a staging environment hinges on the way staging is standardized across the company.

Full staging

There are several ways that the staging phase of the deployment pipeline can be configured. The first is *full staging* (Figure 3-3), where a separate staging ecosystem is running as a complete mirror copy of the entire production ecosystem (though not necessarily with host parity). Full staging still runs on the same core infrastructure as production, but there are several key differences. Staging environments of the services are, at the very least, made accessible to other services by staging-specific frontend and backend ports. Importantly, staging environments in a full-staging ecosystem communicate *only with the staging environments of other services*, and never send any requests or receive any responses from any services running in production (which means sending traffic to production ports from staging is off limits).

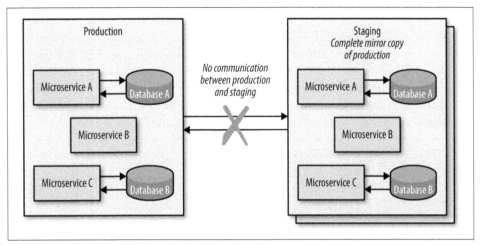

Figure 3-3. Full staging

Full staging requires every microservice to have a fully functional staging environment that other microservices can communicate with when new releases are deployed. Communicating with other microservices within the staging ecosystem can be accomplished either by writing specific tests that are kicked off when a new build is deployed to the staging environment, or as mentioned, by running old recorded production traffic or mock traffic through the service being deployed along with all upstream and downstream dependencies.

Full staging also requires careful handling of test data: staging environments should *never* have write access to any production databases, and granting read access to production databases is discouraged as well. Because full staging is designed to be a complete mirror copy of production, every microservice staging environment should contain a separate test database that it can read from and write to.

Risks of Full Staging

Caution needs to be taken when implementing and deploying full staging environments, because new releases of services will almost always be communicating with other new releases of any upstream and downstream dependencies—this may not be an accurate reflection of the real world. Engineering organizations may need to require teams to coordinate and/or schedule deployments to staging to avoid the deployment of one service breaking the staging environment for all other related services.

Partial staging

The second type of staging environment is known as *partial staging*. As the name suggests, it is not a complete mirror copy of the production environment. Rather, each microservice has its own staging environment, which is a pool of servers with (at the very least) staging-specific frontend and backend ports, and when new builds are introduced into the staging phase, they communicate with the upstream clients and downstream dependencies that are running in production (Figure 3-4).

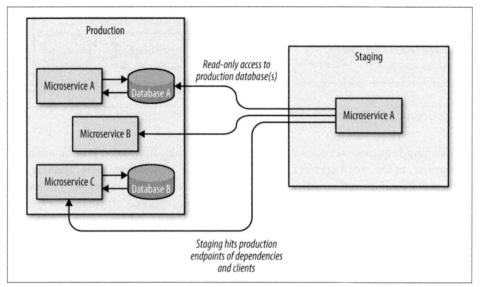

Figure 3-4. Partial staging

Partial staging deployments should hit all production endpoints of a microservice's clients and dependencies to mimic the state of the actual world as accurately as possible. Specific staging tests will need to be written and run to accomplish this, and every new feature added should probably be accompanied by at least one additional staging test to ensure that it is tested thoroughly.

Risks of Partial Staging

Because microservices with partial staging environments communicate with production microservices, extreme care must be taken. Even though partial staging is restricted to read-only requests, production services can easily be taken down by bad staging deploys that send bad requests and/or overload production services with too many requests.

These types of staging environments should also be restricted to read-only database access: a staging environment should never write to a production database. However, some microservices may be very write-heavy, and testing the write functionality of a new build will be essential. The most common way of doing this is to mark any data written by a staging environment as *test data* (this is known as *test tenancy*), but the safest way to do this is to write to a separate test database, since giving write access to a staging environment still runs the risk of altering real-world data. See Table 3-1 for a comparison of full and partial staging environments.

Table 3-1. Full versus partial staging environments

	Full staging	Partial staging
Complete copy of production environment	Yes	No
Separate staging frontend and backend ports	Yes	Yes
Access to production services	No	Yes
Read access to production databases	No	Yes
Write access to production databases	No	Yes
Requires automated rollbacks	No	Yes

Staging environments (full or partial) should have dashboards, monitoring, and logging just like production environments—all of which should be set up identically to the dashboards, monitoring, and logging of the production environment of the microservice (see Chapter 6, *Monitoring*). The graphs for all key metrics can be kept on the same dashboard as all production metrics, though teams may opt to have separate dashboards for each part of the deployment process: a staging dashboard, a canary dashboard, and a production dashboard. Depending on how dashboards are configured, it may be best to keep all graphs for all deployments on one dashboard and to organize them by deployment (or by metric). Regardless of how a team decides to set up their dashboards, the goal of building good and useful production-ready dashboards should not be forgotten: the dashboard(s) of a production-ready microservice should make it easy for an outsider to quickly determine the health and status of the service.

Monitoring and logging for the staging environment should be identical to the monitoring and logging of the staging and production deployments so that any failures of tests and errors in new releases that are deployed to staging will be caught before they move to the next phase of the deployment pipeline. It's extremely helpful to set up alerts and logs so that they are differentiated and separated by deployment type, ensuring that any alerts triggered by failures or errors will specify which environment is experiencing the problem, making debugging, mitigation, and resolution of any bugs or failures rather easy and straightforward.

The purpose of a staging environment is to catch any bugs introduced by code changes before they affect production traffic. When a bug is introduced by the code, it will usually be caught in the staging environment (if it is set up correctly). Automated rollbacks of bad deploys are a necessity for partial staging environments (though are not required for full staging environments). Establishing when to revert to a previous build should be determined by various thresholds on the microservice's key metrics.

Since partial staging requires interacting with microservices running in production, bugs introduced by new releases deployed to a partial staging environment can bring down other microservices that are running in production. If there aren't any automated rollbacks in place, mitigating and resolving these problems needs to be done manually. Any steps of the deployment process that need manual intervention are points of failure not only for the microservice itself, but for the entire microservice ecosystem.

The last question a microservice team needs to answer when setting up a staging environment is how long a new release should run on staging before it can be deployed to canary (and, after that, to production). The answer to this question is determined by the staging-specific tests that are run on staging: a new build is ready to move to the next step of the deployment process as soon as all tests have passed without failing.

Canary

Once a new release has successfully been deployed to staging and passed all required tests, the build can be deployed to the next stage in the deployment pipeline: the *canary* environment. The unique name for this environment comes from a tactic used by coal miners: they'd bring canaries with them into the coal mines to monitor the levels of carbon monoxide in the air; if the canary died, they knew that the level of toxic gas in the air was high, and they'd leave the mines. Sending a new build into a canary environment serves the same purpose: deploy it to a small pool of servers running production traffic (around 5%–10% of production capacity), and if it survives, deploy to the rest of the production servers.

Canary Traffic Distribution

If the production service is deployed in multiple different datacenters, regions, or cloud providers, then the canary pool should contain servers in each of these in order to accurately sample production.

Since a canary environment serves production traffic, it should be considered part of production. It should have the same backend and frontend ports, and canary hosts should be chosen at random from the pool of production servers to ensure accurate sampling of production traffic. Canaries can (and should) have full access to production services: they should hit all production endpoints of upstream and downstream dependencies, and they should have both read and write access to any databases (if applicable).

As with staging, the dashboards, monitoring, and logging should be the same for canaries as for production. Alerts and logs should be differentiated and labeled as coming from the canary deployment so that developers can easily mitigate, debug, and resolve any problems.

Separate Ports for Canaries and Production

Allocating separate frontend and backend ports for canaries and production so that traffic can be directed deliberately may seem like a good idea, but unfortunately separating out the traffic in this fashion defeats the purpose of canaries: to randomly sample production traffic on a small pool of servers to test a new release.

Automated rollbacks absolutely need to be in place for canaries: if any known errors occur, the deployment system needs to automatically revert to the last known stable version. Remember, canaries are serving production traffic, and any problems that happen are affecting the real world.

How long should a new release sit in the canary pool until developers can be satisfied that it is ready for production? This can be minutes, hours, or even days, and the answer is determined by the microservice's traffic patterns. The traffic of every microservice is going to have some sort of pattern, no matter how strange your microservice or business may be. A new release should not leave the canary stage of deployment until a full traffic cycle has been completed. How a "traffic cycle" is defined needs to be standardized across the entire engineering organization, but the duration and requirements of the traffic cycle may need to be created on a service-by-service basis.

Production

Production is the real world. When a build has successfully made it through the development cycle, survived staging, and lived through the coal mines of the canary phase, it is ready to be rolled out to the production deployment. At this point in the deployment pipeline—the very last step—the development team should be completely confident in the new build. Any errors in the code should have been discovered, mitigated, and resolved before making it this far.

Every build that makes it to production should be completely stable and reliable. A build being deployed to production should have already been thoroughly tested, and a build should *never* be deployed to production until it has made it through the staging and canary phases without any issues. Deploying to production can be done in one fell swoop after the build has lived through the canaries, or it can be gradually rolled out in stages: developers can choose to roll out to production by percentage of hardware (e.g., first to 25% of all servers, then to 50%, then 75%, and finally 100%), or by datacenter, or by region, or by country, or any mixture of these.

Enforcing Stable and Reliable Deployment

By the time a new candidate for production has made it through the development process, has survived the staging environment, and has been deployed to the canary phase successfully, the chances of it causing a major outage are very slim, because most bugs in the code will have been caught before the candidate for production is rolled out to production. This is precisely why having a comprehensive deployment pipeline is essential for building a stable and reliable microservice.

For some developers, the delay introduced by the deployment pipeline might seem like an unnecessary burden because it delays their code changes and/or new features from being deployed straight to production minutes after they have been written. In reality, the delay introduced by the phases of the deployment pipeline is very short and easily customizable, but sticking to the standardized deployment process needs to be enforced to ensure reliability. Deploying to a microservice multiple times per day can (and does) compromise the stability and reliability of the microservice and any other services within its complex dependency chain: a microservice that is changing every few hours is rarely a stable or reliable microservice.

Developers may be tempted to skip the staging and canary phases of the deployment process and deploy a fix straight to production if, for example, a serious bug is discovered in production. While this solves the problem quickly, can *possibly* save the company from losing revenue, and can prevent dependencies from experiencing outages, allowing developers to deploy straight to production should be reserved only for the most severe outages. Without these restrictions in place, there is always the unfortunate possibility of abusing the process and deploying straight to production: for most developers, every code change, every deploy is important and may seem important enough to bypass staging and canary, compromising the stability and reliability of the entire microservice ecosystem. When failures occur, development teams should instead be encouraged to always roll back to the latest stable build of the microservice, which will bring the microservice back to a known (and reliable) state, which can run in production without any issues while the team works to discover the root cause of the failure that occurred.

Hotfixes Are an Anti-Pattern

When a deployment pipeline is in place, there should never be any direct deployment to production unless there is an emergency, but even this should be discouraged. Bypassing the initial phases of the deployment pipeline often introduces new bugs into production, as emergency code fixes run the risk of not being properly tested. Rather than deploying a hotfix straight to production, developers should roll back to the latest stable build if possible.

Stable and reliable deployment isn't limited only to following the deployment pipeline, and there are several cases in which blocking a particular microservice from deploying can increase availability across the ecosystem.

If a service isn't meeting their SLAs (see Chapter 2, *Production-Readiness*), all deployment can be postponed if the downtime quota of the service has been used up. For example, if a service has an SLA promising 99.99% availability (allowing 4.38 minutes of downtime each month), but has been unavailable for 12 minutes in one month, then new deployments of that microservice can be blocked for the next three months, ensuring that it meets its SLA. If a service fails load testing (see Chapter 5, *Fault Tolerance and Catastrophe-Preparedness*), then deployment to production can be locked until the service is able to appropriately pass any necessary load tests. For business-critical services, whose outages would stop the company from functioning properly, it can at times be necessary to block deployment if they do not meet the production-readiness criteria established by the engineering organization.

Dependencies

The adoption of microservice architecture is sometimes driven by the idea that microservices can be built and run in isolation, as fully independent and replaceable components of a larger system. This is true in principle, but in the real world, every microservice has *dependencies*, both upstream and downstream. Every microservice will receive requests from *clients* (other microservices) that are counting on the service to perform as expected and to live up to its SLAs, as well as downstream dependencies (other services) that it will depend on to get the job done.

Building and running production-ready microservices requires developers to plan for dependency failures, to mitigate them, and to protect against them. Understanding a service's dependencies and planning for their failures is one of the most important aspects of building a stable and reliable microservice.

To understand how important this is, let's consider an example microservice called *receipt-sender*, whose SLA is four-nines (promising 99.99% availability to upstream clients). Now, *receipt-sender* depends on several other microservices, including one called *customers* (a microservice that handles all customer information), and one called *orders* (a microservice that handles information about the orders each customer places). Both *customers* and *orders* depend on other microservices: *customers* depends on yet another microservice we'll call *customers-dependency*, and *orders* on one we'll refer to as *orders-dependency*. The chances that *customers-dependency* and *orders-dependency* have dependencies of their own are very high, so the dependency graph for *receipt-sender* quickly becomes very, very complicated.

Since *receipt-sender* wants to protect its SLA and provide 99.99% uptime to all of its clients, its team needs to make sure that the SLAs of all downstream dependencies are strictly adhered to. If the SLA of *receipt-sender* depends on *customers* being available 99.99% of the time, but the actual uptime of *customers* is only 89.99% of the time, the availability of *receipt-sender* is compromised and is now only 89.98%. Each one of the dependencies of *receipt-sender* can suffer the same hit to their availability if any of the dependencies in the dependency chain do not meet their SLAs.

A stable and reliable microservice needs to mitigate dependency failures of this sort (and yes, not meeting an SLA is a failure!). This can be accomplished by having backups, fallbacks, caching, and/or alternatives for each dependency just in case they fail.

Before dependency failures can be planned for and mitigated, the dependencies of a microservice must be known, documented, and tracked. Any dependency that could harm a microservice's SLA needs to be included in the architecture diagram and documentation of the microservice (see Chapter 7, *Documentation and Understanding*) and should be included on the service's dashboard(s) (see Chapter 6, *Monitoring*). In addition, all dependencies should be tracked by automatically creating dependency graphs for each service, which can be accomplished by implementing a distributed tracking system across all microservices in the organization.

Once all of the dependencies are known and tracked, the next step is to set up backups, alternatives, fallbacks, or caching for each dependency. The right way to do this is completely dependent on the needs of the service. For example, if the functionality of a dependency can be filled by calling the endpoint of another service, then failure of the primary dependency should be handled by the microservice so that requests are sent to the alternative instead. If requests that need to be sent to the dependency can be held in a queue when the dependency is unavailable, then a queue should be implemented. Another way to handle dependency failures is to put caching for the dependency into place within the service: cache any relevant data so that any failures will be handled gracefully.

The type of cache most often used in these cases is a *Least Recently Used* (LRU) cache, in which relevant data is kept in a queue, and where any unused data is deleted when the cache's queue fills up. LRU caches are easy to implement (often a single line of code for each instantiation), efficient (no expensive network calls need to be made), performant (the data is immediately available), and do a decent job of mitigating any dependency failures. This is known as *defensive caching*, and it is useful for protecting a microservice against the failures of its dependencies: cache the information your microservice gets from its dependencies, and if the dependencies go down, the availability of your microservice will be unaffected. Implementing defensive caching isn't necessary for every single dependency, but if a specific dependency or set of dependencies is or are unreliable, defensive caching will prevent your microservice from being harmed.

Routing and Discovery

Another aspect of building stable and reliable microservices is to ensure that communication and interaction between microservices is itself stable and reliable, which means that layer 2 (the communication layer) of the microservice ecosystem (see Chapter 1, *Microservices*) must be built to perform in a way that protects against harmful traffic patterns and maintains trust across the ecosystem. The relevant parts of the communication layer for stability and reliability (aside from the network itself) are service discovery, service registry, and load balancing.

The *health* of a microservice at both the host level and the service level as a whole should always be known. This means that *health checks* should be running constantly so that a request is never sent to an unhealthy host or service. Running health checks on a separate channel (not used for general microservice communication) is the easiest way to ensure that health checks aren't ever compromised by something like a clogged network. Hardcoding "200 OK" responses on a */health* endpoint for health checks isn't ideal for every microservice either, though it may be sufficient for most. Hardcoded responses don't tell you much except that the microservice was started on the host semi-successfully: any */health* endpoint of a microservice should give a useful, accurate response.

If an instance of a service on a host is unhealthy, the load balancers should no longer route traffic to it. If a microservice as a whole is unhealthy (with all health checks failing on either a certain percentage of hosts or all hosts in production), then traffic should no longer be routed to that particular microservice until the problems causing the health checks to fail are resolved.

However, health checks shouldn't be the only determining factor in whether or not a service is healthy. A large number of unhandled exceptions should also lead to a service being marked unhealthy, and *circuit breakers* should be put into place for these failures so that if a service experiences an abnormal amount of errors, no more requests will be sent to the service until the problem is resolved. The key in stable and reliable routing and discovery is this: preserve the microservice ecosystem by preventing bad actors from serving production traffic and accepting requests from other microservices.

Deprecation and Decommissioning

One often-forgotten, often-ignored cause of instability and unreliability in microservice ecosystems is the *deprecation or decommissioning* of a microservice or one of its API endpoints. When a microservice is no longer in use or is no longer supported by a development team, its decommissioning should be undertaken carefully to ensure that no clients will be compromised. The deprecation of one or more of a microservice's API endpoints is even more common: when new features are added or old ones removed, the endpoints often change, requiring that client teams are updated and any requests made to the old endpoints are switched to new endpoints (or removed entirely).

In most microservice ecosystems, deprecation and decommissioning is more of a sociological problem within the engineering organization than a technical one, making it all the more difficult to address. When a microservice is about to be decommissioned, its development team needs to take care to alert all client services and advise them on how to accommodate the loss of their dependency. If the microservice being decommissioned is being replaced by another new microservice, or if the functionality of the microservice is being built into another existing microservice, then the team should help all clients update their microservices to send requests to the new endpoints. Deprecation of an endpoint follows a similar process: the clients must be alerted, and either given the new endpoint or advised on how to account for the loss of the endpoint entirely. In both deprecation and decommissioning, monitoring plays a critical role: endpoints will need to be monitored closely *before* the service or endpoint is completely decommissioned and/or deprecated to check for any requests that might still be sent to the outdated service or endpoint.

Conversely, failing to properly deprecate an endpoint or decommission a microservice can also have disastrous effects on the microservice ecosystem. This happens more often than developers would care to admit. In an ecosystem containing hundreds or thousands of microservices, developers are often shifted between teams, priorities change, and both microservices and technologies are swapped out for newer, better ones all of the time. When these old microservices or technologies are left to run, without any (or much) involvement, oversight, or monitoring, any failures will go unnoticed, and any failure that is noticed may not be resolved for a long period of time. If a microservice is going to be left to fend for itself, it risks compromising its clients in case of an outage—such microservices should be decommissioned rather than abandoned.

Nothing is more disruptive to a microservice than the complete loss of one of its dependencies. Nothing causes more instability and unreliability than the sudden, unexpected failure of one of its dependencies, even if the failure was planned for by another team. The importance of stable and reliable decommissioning and deprecation can honestly not be emphasized enough.

Evaluate Your Microservice

Now that you have a better understanding of stability and reliability, use the following list of questions to assess the production-readiness of your microservice(s) and microservice ecosystem. The questions are organized by topic, and correspond to the sections within this chapter.

The Development Cycle

- Does the microservice have a central repository where all code is stored?
- Do developers work in a development environment that accurately reflects the state of production (e.g., that accurately reflects the real world)?
- Are there appropriate lint, unit, integration, and end-to-end tests in place for the microservice?
- Are there code review procedures and policies in place?
- Is the test, packaging, build, and release process automated?

The Deployment Pipeline

- Does the microservice ecosystem have a standardized deployment pipeline?
- Is there a staging phase in the deployment pipeline that is either full or partial staging?
- What access does the staging environment have to production services?
- Is there a canary phase in the deployment pipeline?
- Do deployments run in the canary phase for a period of time that is long enough to catch any failures?
- Does the canary phase accurately host a random sample of production traffic?
- Are the microservice's ports the same for canary and production?
- Are deployments to production done all at the same time, or incrementally rolled out?
- Is there a procedure in place for skipping the staging and canary phases in case of an emergency?

Dependencies

- What are this microservice's dependencies?
- What are its clients?

- How does this microservice mitigate dependency failures?
- Are there backups, alternatives, fallbacks, or defensive caching for each dependency?

Routing and Discovery

- Are health checks to the microservice reliable?
- Do health checks accurately reflect the health of the microservice?
- Are health checks run on a separate channel within the communication layer?
- Are there circuit breakers in place to prevent unhealthy microservices from making requests?
- Are there circuit breakers in place to prevent production traffic from being sent to unhealthy hosts and microservices?

Deprecation and Decommissioning

- Are there procedures in place for decommissioning a microservice?
- Are there procedures in place for deprecating a microservice's API endpoints?

CHAPTER 4

Scalability and Performance

A production-ready microservice is scalable and performant. A scalable, performant microservice is one that is driven by efficiency, one that can not only handle a large number of tasks or requests at the same time, but can handle them efficiently and is prepared for tasks or requests to increase in the future. In this chapter, the essential components of microservice scalability and performance are covered, including understanding the qualitative and quantitative growth scales, hardware efficiency, identification of resource requirements and bottlenecks, capacity awareness and planning, scalable handling of traffic, the scaling of dependencies, task handling and processing, and scalable data storage.

Principles of Microservice Scalability and Performance

Efficiency is of the utmost importance in real-world, large-scale distributed systems architecture, and microservice ecosystems are no exception to this rule. It's easy to quantify the efficiency of a single system (like a monolithic application), but evaluating the efficiency and achieving greater efficiency in a large ecosystem of microservices, where tasks are sharded out between hundreds (if not thousands) of small services, is incredibly difficult. It's also bounded by the laws of computer architecture and distributed systems, which place limits on the efficiency of large-scale, complex distributed systems: the more distributed your system, and the more microservices you have in place within that system, the less of a difference the efficiency of one microservice will have on the entire system. Standardization of principles that will increase overall efficiency becomes a necessity. Two of our production-readiness standards—*scalability* and *performance*—help to achieve this overall efficiency, and increase the availability of the microservice ecosystem.

Scalability and performance are uniquely intertwined because of the effects they have on the efficiency of each microservice and the ecosystem as a whole. As we saw in

Chapter 1, *Microservices*, in order to build a scalable application, we need to design for concurrency and partitioning: concurrency allows each task to be broken up into smaller pieces, while partitioning is essential for allowing these smaller pieces to be processed in parallel. So, while *scalability* is related to how we divide and conquer the processing of tasks, *performance* is the measure of how efficiently the application processes those tasks.

In a growing, thriving microservice ecosystem, where traffic is increasing steadily, each microservice needs to be able to scale with the entire system without suffering from performance problems. To ensure that our microservices are scalable and performant, we need to require several things of each microservice. We need to understand its *growth scale*, both quantitative and qualitative, so that we can prepare for expected growth. We need to use our *hardware resources efficiently*, be aware of *resource bottlenecks and requirements*, and do appropriate *capacity planning*. We need to ensure that a microservice's *dependencies will scale* with it. We need to *manage traffic* in a scalable and performant way. We need to *handle and process tasks* in a performant manner. Last but not least, we need to *store data in a scalable way*.

A Production-Ready Service Is Scalable and Performant

- Its qualitative and quantitative growth scales are known.
- It uses hardware resources efficiently.
- Its resource bottlenecks and requirements have been identified.
- Capacity planning is automated and performed on a scheduled basis.
- Its dependencies will scale with it.
- It will scale with its clients.
- Its traffic patterns are understood.
- Traffic can be re-routed in case of failures.
- It is written in a programming language that allows it to be scalable and performant.
- It handles and processes tasks in a performant manner.
- It handles and stores data in a scalable and performant way.

Knowing the Growth Scale

Determining *how* a microservice scales (at a very high level) is the first step toward understanding how to build and maintain a scalable microservice. There are two aspects to knowing the *growth scale* of a microservice, and they both play important roles in understanding and planning for the scalability of a service. The first is the *qualitative growth scale*, which comes from understanding where the service fits into the overall microservice ecosystem and which key high-level business metrics it will be affected by. The second is the *quantitative growth scale*, which is, as its name suggests, a well-defined, measurable, and quantitative understanding of how much traffic a microservice can handle.

The Qualitative Growth Scale

The natural tendency when trying to determine the growth scale of a microservice is to phrase the growth scale in terms of *requests per second* (RPS) or *queries per second* (QPS) that the service can support, then predicting how many RPS/QPS will be made to the service in the future. The term "requests per second" is generally used when talking about microservices, and "queries per second" when talking about databases or microservices that return data to clients, though in many cases they are interchangeable. This is very important information, but it's useless without additional context—specifically, without the context of where the microservice fits into the overall picture.

In most cases, information about the RPS/QPS a microservice can support is determined by the state of the microservice at the time the growth scale is initially calculated: if the growth scale is calculated by only looking at the current levels of traffic and how the microservice handles the current traffic load, making any inferences about how much traffic the microservice can handle in the future runs the risk of being misguided. There are several approaches one could take to get around this problem, including load testing (testing the microservice with higher loads of traffic), which can present a more accurate picture of the scalability of the service, and analyzing historical traffic data to see how the traffic level grows over time. But there's something very key missing here, something that is an inherent property of microservice architecture—namely, that microservices do not live alone but as part of a larger ecosystem.

This is where the *qualitative growth scale* comes in. Qualitative growth scales allow the scalability of a service to tie in with higher-level business metrics: a microservice may, for example, scale with the number of users, with the number of people who open a phone application ("eyeballs"), or with the number of orders (for a food delivery service). These metrics, these qualitative growth scales, aren't tied to an individual microservice but to the overall system or product(s). At the business level, the organization will have, for the most part, some idea of how these metrics will change over time. When these higher-level business metrics are communicated to engineering teams, developers can interpret them as they relate to their respective microservices: if one of their microservices is part of the order flow for a food delivery service, they will know that any metrics related to the number of orders expected in the future will tell them what kind of traffic their service should expect.

When I ask microservice development teams if they know the growth scale of their service, the usual response is, "It can handle x requests per second." My follow-up questions are always geared toward discovering where the service in question fits into the overall product: When are requests made? Is it one request per trip? One request each time someone opens the app? One request every time a new user signs up for our product? When these context-filling questions are answered, the growth scale becomes clear—and useful. If the number of requests made to the service is directly linked to the number of people who open a phone application, then the service scales with eyeballs, and we can plan for scaling the service by predicting how many people will be opening the application. If the number of requests made to the service is determined by the number of people who order delivery food, then the service scales with deliveries, and we can plan and predict for scaling our service by using higher-level business metrics about how many future deliveries are predicted.

There are exceptions to the rules of qualitative growth scales, and determining an appropriate qualitative growth scale can become very complicated the further down the stack the service is found. Internal tools tend to suffer from these complications, and yet they tend to be so business-critical that if they aren't scalable, the rest of the organization quickly hits scalability challenges. It's not easy to put the growth scale of a service like a monitoring or alerting platform in terms of business metrics (users, eyeballs, etc.), so platform and/or infrastructure organizations need to determine accurate growth scales for their services in terms of their customers (developers, services, etc.) and their customers' specifications. Internal tools can scale with, for example, number of deployments, number of services, number of logs aggregated, or gigabytes of data. These are more complicated because of the inherent difficulty in predicting these numbers, but they must be just as straightforward and predictable as the growth scales of microservices higher in the stack.

The Quantitative Growth Scale

The second part of knowing the growth scale is determining its quantitative aspects, which is where RPS/QPS and similar metrics come into play. To determine the *quantitative growth scale*, we need to approach our microservices with the qualitative growth scale in mind: the quantitative growth scale is defined by translating the qualitative growth scale into a measurable quantity. For example, if the qualitative growth scale of our microservice is measured in "eyeballs" (e.g., how many people open a phone application), and each "eyeball" results in two requests to our microservice and one database transaction, then our quantitative growth scale is measured in terms of requests and transactions, resulting in requests per second and transactions per second as the two key quantities determining our scalability.

The importance of choosing accurate qualitative and quantitative growth scales cannot be overemphasized. As we will soon see, the growth scale will be used when making predictions about the service's operational costs, hardware needs, and limitations.

Efficient Use of Resources

When considering the scalability of large-scale distributed systems like microservice ecosystems, one of the most useful abstractions we can make is to treat properties of our hardware and infrastructure systems as *resources*. CPU, memory, data storage, and the network are similar to resources in the natural world: they are finite, they are physical objects in the real world, and they must be distributed and shared between various key players in the ecosystem. As we discussed briefly in "Organizational Challenges" on page 20, hardware resources are expensive, valuable, and sometimes rare, which leads to fierce competition for resources within the microservice ecosystem.

The organizational challenge of resource allocation and distribution can be alleviated by giving business-critical microservices a greater share of the resources. Resource needs can be prioritized by categorizing various microservices within the ecosystem according to their importance and value to the overall business: if resources are scarce across the ecosystem, the most business-critical services can be given higher priority with regard to resource allocation.

The technical challenge of resource allocation and distribution presents some difficulty, because many decisions need to be made about the first layer (the hardware layer) of the microservice ecosystem. Microservices can be given dedicated hardware so that only one service will run on each host, but this can be rather expensive and an inefficient use of hardware resources. Many engineering organizations opt to share hardware among multiple microservices, and each host will run several different services—a practice that is, in most cases, a more efficient use of hardware resources.

The Dangers of Shared Hardware Resources

While running many different microservices on one machine (that is, sharing machines between microservices) is usually a more efficient use of hardware resources, care must be taken to ensure that the microservices are sufficiently isolated and don't compromise the performance, efficiency, or availability of their neighboring microservices. Containerization (using Docker) along with resource isolation can help prevent microservices from being harmed by badly behaved neighbors.

One of the most effective ways to allocate and distribute hardware resources across a microservice ecosystem is to fully abstract away the notion of a host and replace it with hardware resources using resource abstraction technologies like Apache Mesos. Using this level of resource abstraction allows resources to be allocated dynamically, eliminating many of the pitfalls associated with resource allocation and distribution in large-scale distributed systems like microservice ecosystems.

Resource Awareness

Before hardware resources can be efficiently allocated and distributed to microservices within the microservice ecosystem, it is important to identify the *resource requirements* and *resource bottlenecks* of each microservice. Resource requirements are the specific resources (CPU, RAM, etc.) that each microservice needs; identifying these is essential for running a scalable service. Resource bottlenecks are the scalability and performance limitations of each individual microservice that are dependent on features of its resources.

Resource Requirements

The *resource requirements* of a microservice are the hardware resources the microservice needs in order to run properly, to process tasks efficiently, and to be scaled vertically and/or horizontally. The two most important and relevant hardware resources tend to be, unsurprisingly, CPU and RAM (in multithreaded environments, threads become the third important resource). Determining the resource requirements of a microservice then entails quantifying the CPU and RAM that *one instance* of the service needs in order to run. This is essential for resource abstraction, for resource allocation and distribution, and for determining the overall scalability and performance of the microservice.

Identifying Additional Resource Requirements

While CPU and RAM are the two most common resource requirements, it's important to keep an eye out for other resources that a microservice may need within the ecosystem. These can be hardware resources like database connections or application platform resources like logging quotas. Being aware of the needs of a specific microservice can do a lot to improve scalability and performance.

Calculating the specific resource requirements of a microservice can be a tricky, lengthy process, because there are many relevant factors. The key here, as I mentioned earlier, is to determine what the requirements are for only *one instance* of the service. The most effective and efficient way to scale our service is to scale it horizontally: if our traffic is about to increase, we want to add a few more hosts and deploy our service to those new hosts. In order for us to know how many hosts we need to add, we need to know what our service looks like running on only one host: how much traffic can it handle? how much CPU does it utilize? how much memory? Those numbers will tell us exactly what the resource requirements of our microservice are.

Resource Bottlenecks

We can discover and quantify the performance and scalability limitations of our microservices by identifying *resource bottlenecks*. A resource bottleneck is anything inherent about the way the microservice utilizes its resources that limits the scalability of the application. This could be an infrastructure bottleneck or something within the architecture of the service that prevents it from being scalable. For example, the number of open database connections a microservice needs can be a bottleneck if it nears the connection limit of the database. Another example of a common resource bottleneck is when microservices need to be vertically scaled (rather than horizontally scaled, where more instances/hardware is added) when they experience an increase in traffic: if the only way to scale a microservice is to increase the resources of each instance (more CPU, more memory), then the two principles of scalability (concurrency and partitioning) are abandoned.

Some resource bottlenecks are easy to identify. If your microservice can only be scaled to meet growing traffic by deploying it to machines with more CPU and memory, then you have a scalability bottleneck and need to refactor the microservice so that it can be scaled horizontally rather than vertically, using concurrency and partitioning as your guiding principles.

The Pitfalls of Vertical Scaling

Vertical scaling isn't a sustainable or scalable way to architect microservices. It may appear to work out all right in situations where each microservice has dedicated hardware, but it will not work well with the new hardware abstraction and isolation technologies that are used in the tech world today, like Docker and Apache Mesos. Always optimize for concurrency and partitioning if you want to build a scalable application.

Other resource bottlenecks are not as obvious, and the best way to discover them is to run extensive load testing on the service. We will cover load testing in much greater detail in "Resiliency Testing" on page 89.

Capacity Planning

One of the most important requirements of building a scalable microservice is ensuring that it will have access to necessary and required hardware resources as it scales. Efficiently using resources, planning for growth, and designing a microservice for perfect efficiency and scalability from the ground up is all quickly made useless if no hardware resources are available when the microservice needs to host more production traffic. This challenge is especially relevant for microservices that are optimized for horizontal scalability.

In addition to the technical challenges that accompany this potential problem, engineering organizations are often faced with larger organizational-level and business-relevant issues that come along for the ride: hardware resources cost quite a bit of money, businesses and individual development teams within them have budgets to adhere to, and these budgets (which tend to include hardware) need to be planned for in advance. To ensure that microservices can scale properly when traffic increases, we can perform scheduled *capacity planning*. The principles of capacity planning are pretty straightforward: determine the hardware needs of each microservice in advance, build the needs into the budget, and make sure that the required hardware is reserved.

To determine the hardware needs of each service, we can use the growth scales (both quantitative and qualitative), key business metrics and traffic predictions, the known resource bottlenecks and requirements, and historical data about the microservice's traffic. This is where qualitative and quantitative growth scales come in especially handy, because they allow us to figure out precisely how the scalability behavior of our microservices relate to high-level business predictions. For example, if we know that (1) our microservice scales with unique visitors to the overall product, (2) each unique visitor corresponds to a certain number of requests per second made to our microservice, and (3) that the company predicts that the product will receive 20,000 new unique visitors in the next quarter, then we'll know exactly what our capacity needs will be for the next quarter.

This needs to be built into the budget of each development team, each engineering organization, and each company. Running this exercise on a scheduled basis *before* budgeting is determined can help engineering organizations make sure that hardware resources are never unavailable simply because resource budgeting wasn't completed or prepared for. The important thing here (from both the engineering and business perspectives) is to recognize the cost of inadequate capacity planning: microservices that can't scale properly because of hardware shortages lead to decreased availability within the entire ecosystem, which leads to outages, which costs the company money.

Lead Time for New Hardware Requests

One potential problem that's commonly overlooked by development teams during the capacity planning phase is that the hardware that is needed for the microservice might not exist at the time of planning and may need to be acquired, installed, and configured before any microservices can run on it. Before scheduling capacity planning, take care to find out the exact lead time needed for acquiring new hardware in order to avoid long shortages in critical times, and allow some room for delays in the process.

Once the hardware resources have been secured and dedicated to each microservice, capacity planning is complete. Determining when and how to allocate the hardware after the planning phase is, of course, up to each engineering organization and their development, infrastructure, and operations teams.

Capacity planning can be a really difficult and manual task. Like most manual tasks within engineering, it introduces new modes of failure: manual calculations can be off, and even a small shortage can prove disastrous to business-critical services. Automating the majority of the capacity planning process away from development and operations teams cuts down on potential errors and failures, and a great way to accomplish this is to build and run a capacity planning self-service tool within the application platform layer of the microservice ecosystem.

Dependency Scaling

The scalability of a microservice's dependencies can present a scalability problem of its own. A microservice that is architected, built, and run to be perfectly scalable in every way still faces scalability challenges if it's dependencies cannot scale with it. If even one critical dependency is unable to scale with its clients, then the entire dependency chain suffers. Ensuring that all dependencies will scale with a microservice's expected growth is essential for building production-ready services.

This challenge is relevant to every individual microservice and every part of the microservice ecosystem stack, which means that microservice teams also need to make sure that their service isn't a scalability bottleneck for its clients. In other words, additional complexity is introduced by the rest of the microservice ecosystem. The inevitable additional traffic and growth from a microservice's clients need to be prepared for.

Qualitative Growth Scales and Dependency Scalability

When dealing with incredibly complex dependency chains, making sure that all microservice teams tie the scalability of their services to high-level business metrics (using the qualitative growth scale) can make sure that all services are properly prepared for expected growth, even when cross-team communication becomes difficult.

The problem of dependency scaling is an especially strong argument for the implementation of scalability and performance standards across every part of the microservice ecosystem. Most microservices do not live in isolation. Nearly every single microservice is a small part of large, intertwined, intricate dependency chains. In most cases, scaling the entire overall product, the organization, and the ecosystem effectively requires that each piece of the system scales together with the rest. Having a small number of super efficient, performant, and scalable microservices in a system where the rest of the services aren't held to (and don't meet) the same standards renders the efficiency of the standardized services completely moot.

Aside from standardization across the ecosystem, and holding each microservice development team to high scalability standards, it's important that development teams work together across microservice boundaries to ensure that each dependency chain will scale together. The development teams responsible for any dependencies of a microservice need to be alerted when increases in traffic are expected. Cross-team communication and collaboration are essential here: regularly communicating with clients and dependencies about a service's scalability requirements, status, and any bottlenecks can help to guarantee that any services that rely on each other are prepared for growth and aware of any potential scalability bottlenecks. A strategy that I've used to help teams accomplish this is by holding architecture and scalability overview meetings with teams whose services rely on one another. In these meetings, we cover the architecture of each service and its scalability limitations, then discuss together what needs to be done to scale the entire set of services.

Traffic Management

As services scale, and the number of requests each service must handle grows, a scalable, performant service must also handle traffic intelligently. There are several aspects to managing traffic in a scalable, performant way: first of all, the growth scale (quantitative and qualitative) needs to be used to predict future increases (or decreases) in traffic; second, the traffic patterns must be well understood and prepared for; and third, microservices need to be able to intelligently handle increases in traffic, as well as surges or bursts of traffic.

We've already covered the first aspect earlier in this chapter: understanding the growth scales (both quantitative and qualitative) of a microservice allows us to understand current traffic loads on the service as well as prepare for future traffic growth.

Understanding current traffic patterns helps when interacting with the service on the ground floor in a lot of really interesting ways. When traffic patterns are clearly identified, both in terms of the requests per second sent to the service over time and all key metrics (see Chapter 6, *Monitoring*, for more about key metrics), changes to the service, operational downtimes, and deployments can be scheduled to avoid peak traffic times, cutting down on possible future outages if a bug is deployed and on potential downtime if the microservice is restarted while experiencing peak traffic load. Closely monitoring the traffic in light of the traffic patterns and tuning the monitoring thresholds carefully with the traffic patterns of the microservice in mind can help catch any issues and incidents quickly before they cause an outage or lead to decreased availability (the principles of production-ready monitoring are covered in greater detail in Chapter 6, *Monitoring*).

When we can predict future traffic growth and understand the current and past traffic patterns well enough to know how the patterns will change with expected growth, we can perform load testing on our services to make sure that they behave as we expect under heavier traffic loads. The details of load testing are covered in "Resiliency Testing" on page 89.

The third aspect of traffic management is where things get especially tricky. The way a microservice handles traffic should be scalable, which means it should be prepared for drastic changes in traffic, especially bursts of traffic, handle them carefully, and prevent them from taking down the service entirely. It's easier said than done, because even the most well-monitored, scalable, and performant microservices can experience monitoring, logging, and other general issues if traffic suddenly spikes. These sorts of spikes should be prepared for at the infrastructure level, within all monitoring and logging systems, and by the development team as part of the service's resiliency testing suite.

There's one additional aspect I want to mention that's related to management of traffic between and across various locations. Many microservice ecosystems won't be deployed only in one location, one datacenter, or one city, but rather across multiple datacenters across the country (or even the world). It's not uncommon for datacenters themselves to experience large-scale outages, and when this happens, the entire microservice ecosystem can (and usually will) go down with the datacenter. Distributing and routing traffic appropriately between datacenters is the responsibility of the infrastructure level (in particular, the communication layer) of the microservice ecosystem, but each microservice needs to be prepared to re-route traffic from one datacenter to another without the service experiencing any decreased availability.

Task Handling and Processing

Every microservice in the microservice ecosystem will need to process tasks of some sort. That is, every microservice will be receiving requests from upstream client services who either need some sort of information from the microservice or need the microservice to compute or process something and then return information about that computation or process, and then the microservice will need to fulfill that request (usually by communicating with downstream services in addition to doing some work of its own) and return any requested information or response to the client that sent the request.

Programming Language Limitations

Microservices can accomplish this and play their required role in a myriad of ways, and the ways in which they will perform computations, interact with downstream services, and process various tasks will depend on the language that the service is written in, and consequently, on the architecture of the service (which is, in many ways, determined by the language). For example, a microservice written in Python has a number of ways that it can process various tasks, some of which require the use of asynchronous frameworks (like Tornado) and others which can utilize messaging technologies like RabbitMQ and Celery to efficiently process tasks. For these reasons, a microservice's ability to handle and process tasks in a scalable and performant manner is dictated in part by choice of language.

Beware of Scalability and Performance Limitations of Programming Languages

Many programming languages are not optimized for the performance and scalability requirements of microservice architecture, or do not have scalable or performant frameworks that allow microservices to process tasks efficiently.

Because of the limitations introduced by language choice when it comes to a microservice's ability to process tasks efficiently, language choice becomes extremely important in microservice architecture. To many developers, one of the selling points of the adoption of microservice architecture is the ability to write a microservice in any language, and this is usually true, but with a caveat: programming language constraints need to be taken into account, and language choice should be determined not by whether a language is fashionable or fun (or even whether it is the most common language that the development team is familiar with), but with the performance and scalability limitations of each potential language held as the deciding factors. There is no one "best" language to write a microservice in, but there *are* languages that are better suited than others to certain types of microservices.

Handling Requests and Processing Tasks Efficiently

Language choice aside, production-readiness standardization requires each microservice to be both scalable and performant, which means that microservices need to be able to handle and process a large number of tasks at the same time, handle and process those tasks efficiently, and be prepared for tasks and requests to increase in the future. With this in mind, development teams should be able to answer three basic questions about their microservices: how their microservice processes tasks, how efficiently their microservice processes those tasks, and how their microservice will perform as the number of requests scales.

To ensure scalability and performance, microservices need to process tasks efficiently. In order to do this, they need to have both concurrency and partitioning. Concurrency requires that the service can't have one single process that does all of the work: that process will pick up one task at a time, complete the steps in a specific order, and then move on to the next, which is a relatively inefficient way to process tasks. Instead of architecting our service to use a single process, we can introduce concurrency so that each task is broken up into smaller pieces.

Write Microservices in Programming Languages That Are Optimized for Concurrency and Partitioning

Some languages are better suited for efficient (concurrent and partitioned) task handling and processing than others. When writing a new microservice, make sure that the language the service is being written in won't introduce scalability and performance constraints on the microservices. Microservices that are already written in languages with efficiency limitations can (and should) be rewritten in more appropriate languages, a time consuming but incredibly rewarding task that can drastically improve scalability and performance. For example, if you are optimizing for concurrency and partitioning, and want to use an asynchronous framework to help you accomplish that, writing your service in Python (rather than C++, Java, or Go—three languages built for concurrency and partitioning) is going to introduce a lot of scalability and performance bottlenecks that will be difficult to mitigate.

Taking the smaller pieces of these tasks, we can process them more efficiently using partitioning, where each task is not only broken up into small pieces but can be processed in parallel. If we have a large number of small tasks, we can process then all at the same time by sending them to a set of workers that can process them in parallel. If we need to process more tasks, we can easily scale with the increased demand by adding additional workers to process the new tasks without affecting the efficiency of our system. Together, concurrency and partitioning help ensure that our microservice is optimized for both scalability and partitioning.

Scalable Data Storage

Microservices need to *handle data in a scalable and performant way*. The way in which a microservice stores and handles data can easily become the most significant limitation or constraint that keeps it from becoming scalable and performant: choosing the wrong database, the wrong schema, or a database that doesn't support test tenancy can end up compromising the overall availability of a microservice. Choosing the right database for a microservice is a topic that, like all the other topics covered in this book, is incredibly complex, and we will only scratch the surface in this chapter. In the following sections, we'll take a look at several things to consider when choosing databases in microservice ecosystems, and then at some database challenges that are specific to microservice architecture.

Database Choice in Microservice Ecosystems

Building, running, and maintaining databases in large microservice ecosystems is not an easy task. Some companies adopting microservice architecture opt to allow development teams to choose, build, and maintain their own databases, while others will decide on at least one database option that works for the majority of the microservices at the company, and build a separate team to run and maintain the database(s) so that developers can focus solely on their own microservices.

If we think about microservice architecture as being composed of four separate layers (see "Microservice Architecture" on page 9 for more details) and recognize that, thanks to the Inverse Conway's Law, the engineering organizations of companies that adopt microservice architecture will mirror the architecture of its product, then we can see where the responsibility for choosing the appropriate databases, building them, running them, and maintaining them lies: either in the application platform layer, which would allow databases to be provided as a service to microservice teams, or the microservice layer, where the database used by a microservice is considered part of the service. I've seen both of these setups in practice at various companies, and some work better than others. I've also noticed that one approach to this works particularly well: offering databases as a service within the application platform layer, and then allowing individual microservice development teams to run their own database if the databases offered as part of the application platform do not fit their specific needs.

The most common types of databases are *relational databases* (SQL, MySQL) and *NoSQL databases* (Cassandra, Vertica, MongoDB, and key-value stores like Dynamo, Redis, and Riak). Choosing between a relational database and a NoSQL database, and then choosing the specific appropriate database for a microservice's needs depends on the answers to several questions:

- What are the needed transactions per second of each microservice?
- What type of data does each microservice need to store?
- What is the schema needed by each microservice? And how often will it need to be changed?
- Do the microservices need strong consistency or eventual consistency?
- Are the microservices read-heavy, write-heavy, or both?
- Does the database need to be scaled horizontally or vertically?

Regardless of whether the database is maintained as part of the application platform or by each individual microservice development team, database choice should be driven by the answers to those questions. For example, if the database in question needs to be scaled horizontally, or if reads and writes need to be made in parallel, then a NoSQL database should be chosen, since relational databases struggle with horizontal scaling and parallel reads and writes.

Database Challenges in Microservice Architecture

There are several challenges with databases that are specific to microservice architecture. When databases are shared among microservices, competition for resources kicks in, and some microservices may utilize more than their fair share of the available storage. Engineers building and maintaining shared databases need to design their data storage solutions so that the database can be easily scaled if any of the tenant microservices either require additional space or are running the risk of using up all available space.

Watch Out for Database Connections

Some databases have strict limitations on the number of database connections that can be open simultaneously. Make sure that all connections are closed appropriately to avoid compromising both a service's availability and the availability of the database to all microservices that use it.

Another challenge microservices often face, especially once they've built and standardized stable and reliable development cycles and deployment pipelines, is the handling of test data from end-to-end testing, load testing, and any test writes done in staging. As mentioned in "The Deployment Pipeline" on page 44, the staging phase of the deployment pipeline requires reading and/or writing to databases. If full staging has been implemented, then the staging phase will have its own separate test and staging database, but partial staging requires read and write access to production servers, so great care needs to be taken to ensure that test data is handled appropriately: it needs to be clearly marked as test data (a process known as *test tenancy*), and then all test data must be deleted at regular intervals.

Evaluate Your Microservice

Now that you have a better understanding of scalability and performance, use the following list of questions to assess the production-readiness of your microservice(s) and microservice ecosystem. The questions are organized by topic, and correspond to the sections within this chapter.

Knowing the Growth Scale

- What is this microservice's qualitative growth scale?
- What is this microservice's quantitative growth scale?

Efficient Use of Resources

- Is the microservice running on dedicated or shared hardware?
- Are any resource abstraction and allocation technologies being used?

Resource Awareness

- What are the microservice's resource requirements (CPU, RAM, etc.)?
- How much traffic can one instance of the microservice handle?
- How much CPU does one instance of the microservice require?
- How much memory does one instance of the microservice require?
- Are there any other resource requirements that are specific to this microservice?
- What are the resource bottlenecks of this microservice?
- Does this microservice need to be scaled vertically, horizontally, or both?

Capacity Planning

- Is capacity planning performed on a scheduled basis?
- What is the lead time for new hardware?
- How often are hardware requests made?
- Are any microservices given priority when hardware requests are made?
- Is capacity planning automated, or is it manual?

Dependency Scaling

- What are this microservice's dependencies?
- Are the dependencies scalable and performant?
- Will the dependencies scale with this microservice's expected growth?

- Are dependency owners prepared for this microservice's expected growth?

Traffic Management

- Are the microservice's traffic patterns well understood?
- Are changes to the service scheduled around traffic patterns?
- Are drastic changes in traffic patterns (especially bursts of traffic) handled carefully and appropriately?
- Can traffic be automatically routed to other datacenters in case of failure?

Task Handling and Processing

- Is the microservice written in a programming language that will allow the service to be scalable and performant?
- Are there any scalability or performance limitations in the way the microservice handles requests?
- Are there any scalability or performance limitations in the way the microservice processes tasks?
- Do developers on the microservice team understand how their service processes tasks, how efficiently it processes those tasks, and how the service will perform as the number of tasks and requests increases?

Scalable Data Storage

- Does this microservice handle data in a scalable and performant way?
- What type of data does this microservice need to store?
- What is the schema needed for its data?
- How many transactions are needed and/or made per second?
- Does this microservice need higher read or write performance?
- Is it read-heavy, write-heavy, or both?
- Is this service's database scaled horizontally or vertically? Is it replicated or partitioned?
- Is this microservice using a dedicated or shared database?
- How does the service handle and/or store test data?

Fault Tolerance and Catastrophe-Preparedness

A production-ready microservice is fault tolerant and prepared for any catastrophe. Microservices will fail, they will fail often, and any potential failure scenario can and will happen at some point within the microservice's lifetime. Ensuring availability across the microservice ecosystem requires careful failure planning, preparation for catastrophes, and actively pushing the microservice to fail in real time to ensure that it can recover from failures gracefully.

This chapter covers avoiding single points of failure, common catastrophes and failure scenarios, handling failure detection and remediation, implementing different types of resiliency testing, and ways to handle incidents and outages at the organizational level when failures do occur.

Principles of Building Fault-Tolerant Microservices

The reality of building large-scale distributed systems is that individual components can fail, they will fail, and they will fail often. No microservice ecosystem is an exception to this rule. Any possible failure scenario can and will happen at some point in a microservice's lifetime, and these failures are made worse by the complex dependency chains within microservice ecosystems: if one service in the dependency chain fails, all of the upstream clients will suffer, and the end-to-end availability of the entire system will be compromised.

The only way to mitigate catastrophic failures and avoid compromising the availability of the entire system is to require each microservice within the ecosystem to be *fault tolerant* and *prepared for any catastrophe*.

The first step involved in building a fault-tolerant, catastrophe-prepared microservice is to architect away *single points of failure*. There should never be one piece of the ecosystem whose failure can bring the entire system to a halt, nor should there be any individual piece within the architecture of a microservice that will bring the microservice down whenever it fails. Identifying these single points of failure, both within the microservice and at a layer of abstraction above it, can prevent the most glaring failures from occurring.

Identifying failure scenarios is the next step. Not every failure or catastrophe that befalls a microservice is a glaringly obvious single point of failure that can be architected away. Fault tolerance and catastrophe-preparedness require that a microservice withstand both *internal failures* (failures within the microservice itself) and *external failures* (failures within other layers of the ecosystem). From a host failure to the failure of an entire datacenter, from a database to a service's distributed task queue, the number of ways in which a microservice can be brought down by the failure of one or more of its parts is overwhelming, scaling with the complexity of both the microservice itself and the microservice ecosystem as a whole.

Once single points of failure have been architected away and most (if not all) failure scenarios have been identified, the next step is to test for these failures to see whether or not the microservice can recover gracefully when these failures occur, and determine whether or not it is resilient. The resiliency of a service can be tested very thoroughly through *code testing*, *load testing*, and *chaos testing*.

This step is crucial: in a complex microservice ecosystem, merely architecting away failure is not enough—even the best mitigation strategy can turn out to be completely useless when components begin to fail. The only way to build a truly fault-tolerant microservice is to push it to fail in production by actively, repeatedly, and randomly failing each component that could cause the system to break.

Not all failures can be predicted, so the last steps in building fault-tolerant, catastrophe-prepared microservices are organizational in nature. Failure detection and mitigation strategies need to be in place and should be standardized across each microservice team, and every new failure that a service experiences should be added to the resiliency testing suite to ensure it never happens again. Microservice teams also need to be trained to handle failures appropriately: dealing with outages and incidents (regardless of severity) should be standardized across the engineering organization.

A Production-Ready Service Is Fault Tolerant and Prepared for Any Catastrophe

- It has no single point of failure.
- All failure scenarios and possible catastrophes have been identified.
- It is tested for resiliency through code testing, load testing, and chaos testing.
- Failure detection and remediation has been automated.
- There are standardized incident and outage procedures in place within the microservice development team and across the organization.

Avoiding Single Points of Failure

The first place to look for possible failure scenarios is within the architecture of each microservice. If there is one piece of the service's architecture that would bring down the entire microservice if it were to fail, we refer to it as a *single point of failure* for the microservice. No one piece of a microservice's architecture should be able to bring down the service, but they frequently do. In fact, most microservices in the real world don't have just one *single* point of failure but have *multiple* points of failure.

Example: Message Broker as a Single Point of Failure

To understand what a single point of failure would look like in the real production world, let's consider a microservice written in Python that uses a combination of Redis (as message broker) and Celery (as task processor) for distributed task processing.

Let's say that the Celery workers (which are processing the tasks) break down for some reason and are unable to complete any of their work. This isn't necessarily a point of failure, because Redis (acting as the message broker) can retry the tasks when the workers are repaired. While the workers are down, Redis stays up, and the tasks build up in the queue on Redis, waiting to be distributed to the Celery workers once they are back up and running. This microservice, however, hosts a *lot* of traffic (receiving thousands of requests per second), and the queues begin to back up, filling up the entire capacity of the Redis machine. Before you know it, the Redis box is out of memory, and you start losing tasks. This sounds bad enough, but the situation can become even worse than it might at first appear, because your hardware might be shared between many different microservices, and now every other microservice that is using this Redis box as a message broker is losing all of their tasks.

> *This* (the Redis machine in this example) is a single point of failure, and it's a real-world example I've seen many, many time in my experience of working with developers to identify single points of failure in their microservices.

It's easy to identify points of failure within microservices when they actually fail, and we need to fix them in order to bring the microservice back up. Waiting for the failure, however, isn't the best approach if we want our microservices to be fault tolerant and preserve their availability. A great way to discover points of failure before they are responsible for an outage is to run architecture reviews with microservice development teams, ask the developers on each team to draw the architecture of their microservice on a whiteboard, and then walk them through the architecture, asking, "What happens if *this* piece of the microservice architecture fails?" (see "Microservice Understanding" on page 125 for more details on architecture reviews and discovering single points of failure).

No Isolated Points of Failure

Due to the complex dependency chains that exist between different microservices within a microservice ecosystem, a point of failure in the architecture of one individual microservice is often a point of failure for the entire dependency chain, and in extreme cases, for the entire ecosystem. There are no isolated points of failure within microservice ecosystems, which makes identifying, mitigating, and architecting away points of failure essential for achieving fault-tolerance.

Once any single (or multiple) points of failure have been identified, they need to be mitigated, and (if possible) architected away. If the point of failure can be completely architected away and replaced by something more fault tolerant, then the problem is solved. Sadly, we can't always avoid every single way in which a service can fail, and there are some situations in which we can't architect away even the most glaringly obvious points of failure. For example, if our engineering organization mandates the use of a certain technology that works well for the rest of the development teams but represents a single point of failure for our service, then there may not be a way to architect it away, and our only option for bringing our service toward a fault-tolerant state is to find ways of mitigating any negative consequences of its failure.

Catastrophes and Failure Scenarios

If we know anything about complex systems and large-scale distributed system architecture, it's this: that the system will break in any way that it can be broken, and any failure that could possibly happen will almost assuredly happen at some point during the system's lifetime.

Microservices are complex systems. They are part of large-scale distributed systems (microservice ecosystems) and are therefore no exception to this rule. Any possible failure and any possible catastrophe will almost assuredly happen at some point in between the time a microservice's request for comments (RFC) is written up and the time the microservice is being deprecated and decommissioned. Catastrophes happen all of the time: racks fail in datacenters, HVAC systems break, production databases are deleted by accident (yes, this happens more than most developers would like to admit), natural disasters wipe out entire datacenters. Any failure that can happen will happen: dependencies will fail, individual servers will fail, libraries will become corrupted or lost entirely, monitoring will fail, logs can and will be lost (seemingly vanishing into thin air).

Once we've identified, mitigated, and (if possible) architected away any glaringly obvious points of failures in our microservice's architecture, the next step is to *identify any other failure scenarios and potential catastrophes* that could befall our microservice. We can separate these types of failures and catastrophes into four main categories, organizing them using their place in the microservice ecosystem stack. The most common catastrophes and failure scenarios are hardware failures, infrastructure (communication-layer and application-platform-layer) failures, dependency failures, and internal failures. We'll look closely at some of the most common possible failure scenarios within each of these categories in the following sections, but first we'll cover a few common causes of failures that affect every level of the microservice ecosystem.

I should note that the lists of possible failure scenarios presented here are not exhaustive. The objective here is to present the most common scenarios and encourage the reader to determine what sorts of failures and catastrophes their microservice(s) and microservice ecosystem(s) may be susceptible to, and then (where necessary) refer the reader to other chapters within this book where some of the relevant topics are covered. Most of the failures here can be avoided by adopting the production-readiness standards (and implementing their corresponding requirements) found throughout this book, so I've only mentioned a few of the failures, and haven't included every failure that's covered in the other chapters.

Common Failures Across an Ecosystem

There are some failures that happen at every level of the microservice ecosystem. These sorts of failures are usually caused (in some way or other) by the lack of standardization across an engineering organization, because they tend to be operational (and not necessarily technical) in nature. Referring to them as "operational" doesn't mean that they are less important or less dangerous than technical failures, nor does it mean that resolving these failures isn't within the technical realm and isn't the responsibility of microservice development teams. These types of failures tend to be the most serious, have some of the most debilitating technical consequences, and reflect a lack of alignment across the various engineering teams within an organization. Of these types of failures, the most common are insufficient design reviews of system and service architecture, incomplete code reviews, poor development processes, and unstable deployment procedures.

Insufficient design reviews of system and microservice architecture lead to poorly designed services, especially within large and complex microservice ecosystems. The reason for this is simple: no one engineer and no one microservice development team will know the details of the infrastructure and the complexity of all four levels of the ecosystem. When new systems are being designed, and new microservices are being architected, it's vital to the future fault tolerance of the system or service that engineers from each level of the microservice ecosystem are brought into the design process to determine how the system or service should be built and run given the intricacies of the entire ecosystem. However, even if this is done properly when the system or service is first being designed, microservice ecosystems evolve so quickly that the infrastructure is often practically unrecognizable after a year or two, and so scheduled reviews of the architecture with experts from each part of the organization can help to ensure that the system or microservice is up-to-date and fits into the overall ecosystem appropriately. For more details on architecture reviews, see Chapter 7, *Documentation and Understanding*.

Incomplete code reviews are another common source of failure. Even though this problem is not specific to microservice architecture, the adoption of microservice architecture tends to exacerbate the problem. Given the higher developer velocity that comes along with microservices, developers are often required to review any new code written by their teammates several times each day in addition to writing their own code, attending meetings, and doing everything else that they need to accomplish to run their service(s). This requires constant context-switching, and it's easy to lose attention to details within someone else's code when you barely have enough time to review your own before deploying it. This leads to countless bugs being introduced into production, bugs that cause services and systems to fail, bugs that could have been caught with better code review. There are several ways to mitigate this, but it can't ever be completely resolved in an environment with high developer velocity. Care needs to be taken to write extensive tests for each system and service, to test each new change extensively before it hits production, and to ensure that, if bugs aren't caught before they are deployed, they're caught elsewhere in the development process or in the deployment pipeline, which leads us to our next two common causes of failure.

One of the leading causes of outages in microservice ecosystems are bad deployments. "Bad" deployments are those that contain bugs in the code, broken builds, etc. Poor development processes and unstable deployment procedures allow failures to be introduced into production, bringing down any system or service that the failure-inducing problem is deployed to along with any (and sometimes all) of its dependencies. Putting good code review procedures into place, and creating an engineering culture where both code review is taken seriously and developers are given adequate time to focus on reviewing their teammates' code is the first step toward avoiding these kinds of failures, but many of them will still go uncaught: even the best code reviewers can't predict exactly how a code change or new feature will behave in production without further testing. The only way to catch these failures before they bring the system or service down is to build stable and reliable development processes and deployment pipelines. The details of building stable and reliable development processes and deployment pipelines are covered in Chapter 3, *Stability and Reliability*.

Summary: Common Failures Across an Ecosystem

The most common failures that happen across all levels of microservice ecosystems are:

- Insufficient design reviews of system and service architecture
- Incomplete code reviews
- Poor development processes
- Unstable deployment procedures

Hardware Failures

The lowest layer of the stack is where the hardware lies. The hardware layer is comprised of the actual, physical computers that all of the infrastructure and application code run on, in addition to the racks the servers are stored in, the datacenters where the servers are running, and in the case of cloud providers, regions and availability zones. The hardware layer also contains the operating system, resource isolation and abstraction, configuration management, host-level monitoring, and host-level logging. (For more details about the hardware layer of the microservice ecosystems, turn to Chapter 1, *Microservices*.)

Much can go wrong within this layer of the ecosystem, and it is the layer that genuine catastrophes (and not just failures) affect the most. It's also the most delicate layer of the ecosystem: if the hardware fails and there aren't alternatives, the entire engineering organization goes down with it. The catastrophes that happen here are pure hardware failures: a machine dies or fails in some way, a rack goes down, or an entire datacenter fails. These catastrophes happen more often than we would like to admit, and in order for a microservice ecosystem to be fault tolerant, in order for any individual microservice to be fault tolerant and prepared for these catastrophes, these failures need to be planned for, mitigated, and protected against.

Everything else within this layer that lies on top of the bare machines can fail, too. Machines need to be provisioned before anything can run on them, and if provisioning fails, then utilizing any new machines (or, in some cases, even old machines) won't be able to happen. Many microservice ecosystems that utilize technologies that support resource isolation (like Docker) or resource abstraction and allocation (like Mesos and Aurora) can also break or fail, and their failures can bring the entire ecosystem to a halt. Failures caused by broken configuration management or configuration changes are extraordinarily common as well, and are often difficult to detect. Monitoring and logging can fail miserably here as well, and if host-level monitoring and logging fails in some way, triaging any outages becomes impossible because the data needed to mitigate any problems won't be available. Network failures (both internal and external) can also happen. Finally, operational downtimes of critical hardware components—even if communicated properly throughout the organization —can lead to outages across the ecosystem.

Summary: Common Hardware Failure Scenarios

Some of the most common hardware failure scenarios are:

- Host failure
- Rack failure
- Datacenter failure
- Cloud provider failure
- Server provisioning failure
- Resource isolation and/or abstraction technology failure
- Broken configuration management
- Failures caused by configuration changes
- Failures and gaps in host-level monitoring
- Failures and gaps in host-level logging
- Network failure
- Operational downtimes
- Lack of infrastructure redundancy

Communication-Level and Application Platform–Level Failures

The second and third layers of the microservice ecosystem stack are comprised of the communication and application platform layers. These layers live between the hardware and the microservices, bridging the two as the glue that holds the ecosystem together. The communication layer contains the network, DNS, the RPC framework, endpoints, messaging, service discovery, service registry, and load balancing. The application platform layer is comprised of the self-service development tools, development environment, test and package and release and build tools, the deployment pipeline, microservice-level logging, and microservice-level monitoring—all critical to the day-to-day running and building of the microservice ecosystem. Like hardware failures, failures that happen at these levels compromise the entire company, because every aspect of development and maintenance within the microservice ecosystem depends critically on these systems running smoothly and without failure. Let's take a look at some of the most common failures that can happen within these layers.

Within the communication layer, network failures are especially common. These can be failures of the internal network(s) that all remote procedure calls are made over, or failures of external networks. Another type of network-related failure arises from problems with firewalls and improper iptables entries. DNS errors are also quite common: when DNS errors happen, communication can grind to a halt, and DNS bugs can be rather difficult to track down and diagnose. The RPC layer of communication —the glue that holds the entire delicate microservice ecosystem together—is another (rather infamous) source of failure, especially when there is only one channel connecting all microservices and internal systems; setting up separate channels for RPC and health checks can mitigate this problem a bit if health checks and other related monitoring is kept separate from channels that handle data being passed between services. It's possible for messaging systems to break (as I mentioned briefly in the Redis-Celery example earlier in this chapter), and messaging queues, message brokers, and task processors often live in microservice ecosystems without any backups or alternatives, acting as frightening points of failure for every service that relies on them. Failures of service discovery, service registry, and load balancing can (and do) happen as well: if any part of these systems breaks or experiences downtime without any alternatives, then traffic won't be routed, allocated, and distributed properly.

Failures within the application platform are more specific to the way that engineering organizations have set up their development process and deployment pipeline, but as a rule, these systems can fail just as often and as catastrophically as every other service within the ecosystem stack. If development tools and/or environments are working incorrectly when developers are trying to build new features or repair existing bugs, bugs and new failure modes can be introduced into production. The same goes for any failures or shortcomings of the test, package, build, and release pipelines: if packages and builds contain bugs or aren't properly put together, then deployments will fail. If the deployment pipeline is unavailable, buggy, or fails outright, then deployment will grind to a halt, preventing not only deployment of new features but of critical bug-fixes that may be in the works. Finally, monitoring and logging of individual microservices can contain gaps or fail as well, making triaging or logging any issues impossible.

Summary: Common Communication and Application Platform Failures

Some of the most common communication and application platform failures are:

- Network failures
- DNS errors
- RPC failures
- Improper handling of requests and/or responses
- Messaging system failures
- Failures in service discovery and service registry
- Improper load balancing
- Failure of development tools and development environment
- Failures in the test, package, build, and release pipelines
- Deployment pipeline failures
- Failures and gaps in microservice-level logging
- Failures and gaps in microservice-level monitoring

Dependency Failures

Failures within the top level of the microservice ecosystem (the microservice layer) can be divided into two separate categories: (1) those that are internal to a specific microservice and caused by problems within it, and (2) those that are external to a microservice and caused by the microservice's dependencies. We'll cover common failure scenarios within this second category first.

Failures and outages of a downstream microservice (that is, one of a microservice's dependencies) are extraordinarily common and can dramatically affect a microservice's availability. If even one microservice in the dependency chain goes down, it can take all of its upstream clients down with it if there are no protections in place. However, a microservice doesn't always necessarily need to experience a full-blown outage in order to negatively affect the availability of its upstream clients—if it fails to meet its SLA by just one or two nines, the availability of all upstream client microservices will drop.

The True Expense of Unmet SLAs

Microservices can cause their upstream clients to fail to meet their SLAs. If a service's availability drops by one or two nines, all upstream clients suffer, all thanks to how the math works: the availability of a microservice is calculated as its own availability multiplied by the availability of its downstream dependencies. Failing to meet an SLA *is* an important (and often overlooked) microservice failure, and it's a failure that brings down the availability of every other service that depends on it (along with the services that depend on those services).

Other common dependency failures are those caused by timeouts to another service, the deprecation or decommissioning of a dependency's API endpoints (without proper communication regarding the deprecation or decommissioning to all upstream clients), and the deprecation or decommissioning of an entire microservice. In addition, versioning of internal libraries and/or microservices and pinning to specific versions of internal libraries and/or services is very much discouraged in microservice architecture because it tends to lead to bugs and (in extreme cases) serious failures, because of the fast-paced nature of microservice development: these libraries and services are constantly changing, and pinning to specific versions (along with versioning of these services and libraries in general) can lead to developers using unstable, unreliable, and sometimes unsafe versions of them.

Failures of external dependencies (third-party services and/or libraries) can and do happen as well. These can be more difficult to detect and fix than failures of internal dependencies, because developers will have little to no control over them. The complexity associated with depending on third-party services and/or libraries can be handled properly if these scenarios are anticipated from the beginning of the microservice's lifecycle: choose established and stable external dependencies, and try to avoid using them unless completely necessary, lest they become a single point of failure for your service.

Summary: Common Dependency Failure Scenarios

Some of the most common dependency failure scenarios are:

- Failures or outages of a downstream (dependency) microservice
- Internal service outages
- External (third-party) service outages
- Internal library failures
- External (third-party) library failures
- A dependency failing to meet its SLA

- API endpoint deprecation
- API endpoint decommissioning
- Microservice deprecation
- Microservice decommissioning
- Interface or endpoint deprecation
- Timeouts to a downstream service
- Timeouts to an external dependency

Internal (Microservice) Failures

At the very top of the microservice ecosystem stack lie the individual microservices. To the development teams, these are the failures that matter the most, because they are completely dependent on good development practices, good deployment practices, and the ways in which development teams architect, run, and maintain their individual microservices.

Assuming that the infrastructure below the microservice layer is relatively stable, the majority of incidents and outages experienced by a microservice will be almost solely self-inflicted. Developers on call for their services will find themselves paged almost solely for issues and failures whose root causes are found within their microservice— that is, the alerts they will receive will have been triggered by changes in their microservice's key metrics (see Chapter 6, *Monitoring*, for more information about monitoring, logging, alerting, and microservice key metrics).

Incomplete code reviews, lack of proper test coverage, and poor development processes in general (specifically, the lack of a standardized development cycle) lead to buggy code being deployed to production—failures that can be avoided by standardizing the development process across microservice teams (see "The Development Cycle" on page 42). Without a stable and reliable deployment pipeline containing staging, canary, and production phases in place to catch any errors before they are fully rolled out to production servers, any problems not caught by testing in the development phases can cause serious incidents and outages for the microservice itself, its dependencies, and any other parts of the microservice ecosystem that depend on it.

Anything specific to the microservice's architecture can also fail here, including any databases, message brokers, task-processing systems, and the like. This is also where general and specific code bugs within the microservice will cause failures, as well as improper error and exception handling: unhandled exceptions and the practice of catching exceptions are an often-overlooked culprit when microservices fail. Finally, increases in traffic can cause a service to fail if the service isn't prepared for unexpected growth (for more on scalability limitations, turn to Chapter 4, *Scalability and Performance*, and then read "Load Testing" on page 91 of the current chapter).

Summary: Common Microservice Failure Scenarios

Some of the most common microservice failures are:

- Incomplete code reviews
- Poor architecture and design
- Lack of proper unit and integration tests
- Bad deployments
- Lack of proper monitoring
- Improper error and exception handling
- Database failure
- Scalability limitations

Resiliency Testing

Architecting away single points of failure and identifying possible failure scenarios and catastrophes isn't enough to ensure that microservices are fault tolerant and prepared for any catastrophe. In order to be truly fault tolerant, a microservice must be able to experience failures and recover from them gracefully without affecting their own availability, the availability of their clients, and the availability of the overall microservice ecosystem. The single best way to ensure that a microservice is fault tolerant is to take all of the possible failure scenarios that it could be affected by, and then actively, repeatedly, and randomly push it to fail in production—a practice known as *resiliency testing*.

A resilient microservice is one that can experience and recover from failures at every level of the microservice ecosystem: the hardware layer (e.g., a host or datacenter failure), the communication layer (e.g., RPC failures), the application layer (e.g., a failure in the deployment pipeline), and in the microservice layer (e.g., failure of a dependency, a bad deployment, or a sudden increase in traffic). There are several types of resiliency testing that, when used to evaluate the fault tolerance of a microservice, can ensure that the service is prepared for any known failures within any layer of the stack.

The first type of resiliency testing we will look at is *code testing*, which is comprised of four types of tests that check syntax, style, individual components of the microservice, how the components work together, and how the microservice performs within its complex dependency chains. (Code testing usually isn't considered part of the resiliency testing suite, but I wanted to include it here for two reasons: first, since it is crucial for fault tolerance and catastrophe-preparedness, it makes sense to keep it in this section; second, I've noticed that development teams have preferred to keep all testing information in one place.) The second is *load testing*, in which microservices are exposed to higher traffic loads to see how they behave under increased traffic. The third type of resiliency testing is *chaos testing*, which is the most important type of resiliency testing, in which microservices are actively pushed to fail in production.

Code Testing

The first type of resiliency testing is *code testing*, a practice almost all developers and operational engineers are familiar with. In microservice architecture, code testing needs to be run at every layer of the ecosystem, both within the microservices and on any system or service that lives in the layers below: in addition to microservices, service discovery, configuration management, and related systems also need to have proper code testing in place. There are several types of good code testing practices, including *lint testing, unit testing, integration testing*, and *end-to-end testing*.

Lint tests

Syntax and style errors are caught using *lint testing*. Lint tests run over the code, catching any language-specific problems, and also can be written to ensure that code matches language-specific (and sometimes team-specific or organization-specific) style guidelines.

Unit tests

The majority of code testing is done through *unit tests*, which are small and independent tests that are run over various small pieces (or units) of the microservice's code. The goal of unit tests is to make sure that the software components of the service itself (e.g., functions, classes, and methods) are resilient and don't contain any bugs. Unfortunately, many developers only consider unit tests when writing tests for their applications or microservices. While unit testing is good, it's not good enough to evaluate the actual ways in which the microservice will behave in production.

Integration tests

While unit tests evaluate small pieces of the microservice to ensure that the components are resilient, the next type of code tests are *integration tests*, which test how the entire service works. In integration testing, all of the smaller components of the microservice (which were testing individually using unit tests) are combined and tested together to make sure that they work as expected when they need to work together.

End-to-end tests

For a monolithic or standalone application, often unit tests and integration tests are good enough together to comprise the code testing aspect of resiliency testing, but microservice architecture introduces a new level of complexity within code testing due to the complex dependency chains that exist between a microservice, its clients, and its dependencies. Another additional set of tests need to be added to the code testing suite that evaluate the behavior of the microservice with respect to its clients and dependencies. This means that microservice developers need to build *end-to-end tests* that run just like real production traffic, tests that hit the endpoints of their microservice's clients, hit their own microservice's endpoints, hit the endpoints of the microservice's dependencies, send read requests to any databases, and catch any problems in the request flow that might have been introduced with a code change.

Automating code tests

All four types of code tests (lint, unit, integration, and end-to-end) should be written by the development team, but running them should be automated as part of the development cycle and the deployment pipeline. Unit and integration tests should run during the development cycle on an external build system, right after changes have made it through the code review process. If the new code changes fail any unit or integration tests, then they should not be introduced into the deployment pipeline as a candidate for production, but should be rejected and brought to the attention of the development team for repair. If the new code changes pass all unit and integration tests, then the new build should be sent to the deployment pipeline as a candidate for production.

Summary of Code Testing

The four types of production-ready code testing are:

- Lint tests
- Unit tests
- Integration tests
- End-to-end tests

Load Testing

As we saw in Chapter 4, *Scalability and Performance*, a production-ready microservice needs to be both scalable and performant. It needs to handle a large number of tasks or requests at the same time and handle them efficiently, and it also must be prepared for tasks or requests to increase in the future. Microservices that are unprepared for increases in traffic, tasks, or requests can experience severe outages when any of these gradually or suddenly increase.

From the point of view of a microservice development team, we know that traffic to our microservice will mostly likely increase at some time in the future, and we might even know by exactly how much the traffic will increase. We want to be fully prepared for these increases in traffic so that we can avoid any potential problems and/or failures. In addition, we want to illuminate any possible scalability challenges and bottlenecks that we might not be aware of until our microservice is pushed to the very limits of its scalability. To protect against any scalability-related incidents and outages, and to be fully prepared for future increases in traffic, we can test the scalability of our services using *load testing*.

Fundamentals of load testing

Load testing is exactly what its name implies: it is a way to test how a microservice behaves under a specific traffic load. During load testing, a target traffic load is chosen, the target load of test traffic is run on the microservice, and then the microservice is monitored closely to see how it behaves. If the microservice fails or experiences any issues during load testing, its developers will be able to resolve any scalability issues that appear in load tests that would have otherwise harmed the availability of their microservice in the future.

Load testing is where the growth scales and resource bottlenecks and requirements that were covered in Chapter 4, *Scalability and Performance*, come in handy. From a microservice's qualitative growth scale and the associated high-level business metrics, development teams can learn how much traffic their microservice should be prepared to handle in the future. From the quantitative growth scale, developers will know exactly how many requests or queries per second their service will be expected to handle. If the majority of the service's resource bottlenecks and resource requirements have been identified, and the bottlenecks architected away, developers will know how to translate the quantitative growth scale (and, consequently, the quantitative aspects of future increases in traffic) into terms of the hardware resources their microservice will require in order to handle higher traffic loads. Load testing after all of this, after applying the scalability requirements and working through them, can validate and ensure that the microservice is ready for the expected increase in traffic.

Load testing can be used the other way around, to discover the quantitative and qualitative growth scales, to identify resource bottlenecks and requirements, to ensure dependency scaling, to determine and plan for future capacity needs, and the like. When done well, load testing can give developers deep insight into the scalability (and scalability limitations) of their microservice: it measures how the service, its dependencies, and the ecosystem behave in a controlled environment under a specified traffic load.

Running load tests in staging and production

Load testing is most effective when it is run on each stage of the deployment pipeline. To test the load testing framework itself, to make sure that the test traffic produces the desired results, and to catch any potential problems that load testing might cause in production, load testing can be run in the staging phase of the deployment pipeline. If the deployment pipeline is utilizing partial staging, where the staging environment communicates with production services, care needs to be taken to make sure that any load tests run in staging do not harm or compromise the availability of any production services that it communicates with. If the deployment pipeline contains full staging, which is a complete mirror copy of production and where no staging services communicate with any services in production, then care needs to be taken to make sure that load testing in full staging produces accurate results, especially if there isn't host parity between staging and production.

It's not enough to load test only in staging. Even the best staging environments—those that are complete mirror copies of production and have full host parity—still are not production. They're not the real world, and very rarely are staging environments perfectly indicative of the consequences of load testing in production. Once you know the traffic load you need to hit, you've alerted all of the on-call rotations of the dependency teams, and you've tested your load tests in staging, you absolutely need to run load tests in production.

Alert Dependencies When Load Testing

If your load tests send requests to other production services, be sure to alert all dependencies in order to avoid compromising their availability while running load tests. Never assume that downstream dependencies can handle the traffic load you are about to send their way!

Load testing in production can be dangerous and can easily cause a microservice and its dependencies to fail. The reason why load testing is dangerous is the same reason it is essential: most of the time, you won't know exactly how the service being tested behaves under the target traffic load, and you won't know how its dependencies handle increased requests. Load testing is *the* way to explore the unknowns about a service and make sure that it is prepared for expected traffic growth. When a service is pushed to its limits in production, and things begin to break, there need to be automated pieces in place to make sure that any load tests can be quickly shut down. After the limitations of the service have been discovered and mitigated and the fixes have been tested and deployed, load testing can resume.

Automating load testing

If load testing is going to be required for all microservices within the organization (or even just a small number of business-critical microservices), leaving the implementation and methodology of the load testing in the hands of development teams to design and run for themselves introduces another point of failure into the system. Ideally, a self-service load-testing tool and/or system should be part of the application platform layer of the microservice ecosystem, allowing developers to use a trusted, shared, automated, and centralized service.

Load testing should be scheduled regularly, and viewed as an integral component of the day-to-day function of the engineering organization. The scheduling should be linked to traffic patterns: test desired traffic loads in production when traffic is low, and never during peak hours, to avoid compromising the availability of any services. If a centralized self-service load testing system is being used, it is incredibly useful to have an automated process for validating new tests, along with a suite of trusted (and required) tests that every service can run. In extreme cases, and when a self-service load testing tool is reliable, deployments can be blocked (or gated) if a microservice fails to perform adequately under load tests. Most importantly, every load test performed needs to be sufficiently logged and publicized internally so that any problems caused by load testing can quickly be detected, mitigated, and resolved.

Summary of Load Testing

Production-ready load testing has the following components:

- It uses a target traffic load that is calculated using the qualitative and quantitative growth scales and expressed in terms of RPS, QPS, or TPS.
- It is run in each stage of the deployment pipeline.
- Its runs are communicated to all dependencies.
- It is fully automated, is logged, and is scheduled.

Chaos Testing

In this chapter, we've seen various potential failure scenarios and catastrophes that can happen at each layer of the stack. We've seen how code testing catches small potential failures at the individual microservice level, and how load testing catches failures that arise from scalability limitations at the microservice level. However, the majority of the failure scenarios and potential catastrophes lie elsewhere in the ecosystem and cannot be caught by any of these kinds of tests. To test for *all* failure scenarios, to make sure that microservices can gracefully recover from any potential catastrophe, there's one additional type of resiliency testing that needs to be in place, and it's known (quite appropriately) as *chaos testing*.

In chaos testing, microservices are actively *pushed to fail* in production, because the only way to make sure that a microservice can survive a failure is to make it fail all of the time, and in every way possible. That means that every failure scenario and potential catastrophe needs to be identified, and then is needs to be forced to happen in production. Running scheduled and random tests of each failure scenario and potential catastrophe can help mimic the real world of complex system failures: developers will know that part of the system will be pushed to fail on a scheduled basis and will prepare for those scheduled chaos runs, and they'll also be caught off guard by randomly scheduled tests.

Responsible Chaos Testing

Chaos testing must be well controlled in order to avoid chaos tests from bringing down the ecosystem. Make sure your chaos testing software has appropriate permissions, and that every single event is logged, so that if microservices are unable to gracefully recover (or if the chaos testing goes rogue), pinpointing and resolving the problems won't require any serious sleuthing.

Like load testing (and many of the other systems covered in this book), chaos testing is best provided as a service, and not implemented in various ad hoc manners across development teams. Automate the testing, require every microservice to run a suite of both general and service-specific tests, encourage development teams to discover additional ways their service can fail, and then give them the resources to design new chaos tests that push their microservices to fail in these new ways. Make sure that every part of the ecosystem (including the chaos testing service) can survive a standard set of chaos tests, and break each microservice and piece of the infrastructure multiple times, again and again and again, until every development and infrastructure team is confident that their services and systems can withstand inevitable failures.

Finally, chaos testing is not just for companies hosted on cloud providers, even though they are the most vocal (and common) users. There are very few differences in failure modes of bare-metal versus cloud provider hardware, and anything that is built to run in the cloud can work just as well on bare metal (and vice versa). An open source solution like Simian Army (which comes with a standard suite of chaos tests that can be customized) will work for the majority of companies, but organizations with specific needs can easily build their own.

Failure Detection and Remediation

In addition to the resiliency testing suite, in which microservices are tested for every known failure and catastrophe, a production-ready microservice needs to have *failure detection and remediation strategies* for when failures do happen. We'll take a look at organizational processes that can be used across the ecosystem to triage, mitigate, and resolve incidents and outages, but first we'll focus on several technical mitigation strategies in this section.

When a failure does happen, the goal of failure detection and remediation always needs to be the following: *reduce the impact to users*. In a microservice ecosystem, the "users" are whoever may be using the service—this could be another microservice (who is a client of the service) or an actual customer of the product (if the service in question is customer-facing). If the failure in question was (or may have been) introduced into production by a new deployment, the single most effective way to reduce the impact to users when something is going wrong is to immediately roll back to the last stable build of the service. Rolling back to the last stable build ensures that the microservice has been returned to a known state, a state that wasn't susceptible to the failures or catastrophes that were introduced with the newest build. The same holds for changes to low-level configurations: treat configs like code, deploy them in various successive releases, and make sure that if a config change causes an outage, the system can quickly and effortlessly roll back to the last stable set of configurations.

A second strategy in case of failure is failing over to a stable alternative. If one of a microservice's dependencies is down, this would mean sending requests to a different endpoint (if the endpoint is broken) or a different service (if the entire service is down). If it's not possible to route to another service or endpoint, then there needs to be a way to queue or save the requests and hold them until problems with the dependency have been mitigated. If the problem is relegated to one datacenter, or if a datacenter is experiencing failures, the way to fail over to a stable alternative would be to re-route traffic to another datacenter. Whenever you are faced with various ways to handle failure, and one of those choices is to re-route traffic to another service or datacenter, re-routing the traffic is almost always the smartest choice: routing traffic is easy and immediately reduces the impact to users.

Importantly, the detection aspect of "failure detection and remediation" can only really be accomplished by production-ready monitoring (see Chapter 6, *Monitoring*, for all the nitty-gritty monitoring details). Human beings are horrible at detecting and diagnosing system failures, and introducing engineers into the failure detection process becomes a single point of failure for the overall system. This holds for failure remediation as well: most of the remediation within large microservice ecosystems is done by engineers, all by hand, all in an almost painfully manual way, introducing a new point of failure for the system—but it doesn't have to be that way. To cut out the potential and possibility for human error in failure remediation, all mitigation strategies need to be automated. For example, if a service fails certain healthchecks or its key metrics hit the warning and/or critical thresholds after a deploy, then the system can be designed to automatically roll back to the last stable build. The same goes for traffic routing to another endpoint, microservice, or datacenter: if certain key metrics hit specific thresholds, set up a system that automatically routes the traffic for you. Fault tolerance absolutely requires that the potential and possibility for human error be automated and architected away whenever possible.

Incidents and Outages

Throughout this book, I've emphasized the availability of the microservices and the overall ecosystem as the goal of standardization. Architecting, building, and running microservice architecture that is geared toward high availability can be accomplished through adopting the production-readiness standards and their related requirements, and it's the reason I've introduced and chosen each production-readiness standard. It's not enough, however, for the individual microservices and each layer of the microservice ecosystem stack to be fault tolerant and prepared for any catastrophe. The development teams and the engineering organization(s) responsible for the microservices and the ecosystem they live in need to have the appropriate organizational response procedures in place for handling incidents and outages when they happen.

Every minute that a microservice is down brings down its availability. When part of the microservice or its ecosystem fails, causing an incident or outage to happen, every minute that it is down counts against its availability and causes it to fail to meet its SLA. Failing to meet an SLA, and failing to meet availability goals, incurs a serious cost: at most companies, outages mean a huge financial cost to the business, a cost that is usually easy to quantify and share with development teams within the organization. With this in mind, it's easy to see how the length of the time to detection, the time to mitigation, and the time to resolution of outages can add up very quickly and cost the company money, because they count against a microservice's uptime (and, consequently, its availability).

Appropriate Categorization

Not all microservices are created equal, and categorizing the importance and impact that their failures will have on the business makes it easier to properly triage, mitigate, and resolve incidents and outages. When an ecosystem contains hundreds or even thousands of microservices, there will be dozens or even hundreds of failures per week, even if only 10 percent of the microservices experience failures, that's still over 100 failures in an ecosystem of 1,000 services. While every failure needs to be properly handled by its on-call rotation, not every failure will need to be treated as an all-hands-on-deck emergency.

In order to have a consistent, appropriate, effective, and efficient incident and outage response process across the organization, it is important to do two things. First, it is incredibly helpful to categorize the microservices themselves with regard to how their failures will affect the ecosystem so that it will be easy to prioritize various incidents and failures (this also helps with problems related to competition for resources—both engineering resources and hardware resources—within the organization). Second, incidents and outages need to be categorized so that the scope and severity of every single failure will be understood across the organization.

Categorizing microservices

To mitigate the challenges of competition for resources, and to ensure proper incident response measures are taken, each microservice within the ecosystem can (and should) be categorized and ranked according to its criticality to the business. Categorization doesn't need to be perfect at first, as a rough categorization rubric will do the job just fine. The key here is to mark microservices that are critical to the business as having the highest priority and impact, and then every other microservice will have a lower rank and priority depending on how close or far it is to the most critical services. Infrastructure layers are always of the highest priority: anything within the hardware, communication, and application platform layers that is used by any of the business-critical microservices should be the highest priority within the ecosystem.

Categorizing incidents and outages

There are two axes that every incident, outage, and failure can be plotted against: the first is the *severity* of the incident, outage, or failure, and the second is its *scope*. Severity is linked to the categorization of the application, microservice, or system in question. If the microservice is business-critical (i.e., if either the business or an essential customer-facing part of the product cannot function without it), then the severity of any failure it experiences should match the service's categorization. Scope, on the other hand, is related to how much of the ecosystem is affected by the failure, and is usually split into three categories: high, medium, and low. An incident whose scope is high is an incident that affects the entire business and/or an external (e.g., user-facing) feature; a medium-scope incident would be one that affected only the service itself, or the service and a few of its clients; a low-scope incident would be one whose negative effects are not noticed by clients, the business, or external customers using the product. In other words, severity should be categorized based on the impact to the business, and scope should be categorized based on whether the incident is *local* or *global*.

Let's go through a few examples to clarify what this looks like in practice. We'll assign four levels of severity to each failure (0–4, where 0 is the most severe incident level and 4 is the least severe), and we'll stick with the high-medium-low levels when determining scope. First, let's look at an example whose severity and scope are very easy to categorize: a complete datacenter failure. If a datacenter goes completely down (for whatever reason), the severity is clearly 0 (it affects the entire business), and the scope is high (again, it affects the entire business). Now let's look at another scenario: imagine we have a microservice that is responsible for a business-critical function in the product, and it goes down for 30 minutes; as a result of its failure, let's imagine that one of its clients suffers, but the rest of the ecosystem remains unaffected. We'd categorize this as severity 0 (because it impacts a business-critical feature) and scope medium (it doesn't affect the whole business, only itself and one client service). Finally, let's consider an internal tool responsible for generating templates for new microservices, and imagine that it goes down for several hours—how would this be categorized? Generating templates for new microservices (and spinning up new microservices) isn't business-critical and doesn't affect any user-facing features, so this wouldn't be a 0 severity problem (it probably wouldn't be a 1 or a 2 either); however, since the service itself is down, we'd probably categorize its severity as a 3, and then its scope as low (since it is the only service affected by its failure).

The Five Stages of Incident Response

When failures happen, it's critical to the availability of the entire system that there are standardized incident response procedures in place. Having a clear set of steps that need to be taken when an incident or outage occurs cuts down on the time to mitigation and the time to resolution, which in turn decreases the downtime experienced by each microservice. Within the industry today, there are typically three standard steps in the process of responding to and resolving an incident: triage, mitigate, and resolve. Adopting microservice architecture, however, and achieving high availability and fault tolerance requires adopting two additional steps in the incident response process: one for coordination, and another for follow-up. Together, these steps give us the five stages of incident response (Figure 5-1): *assessment, coordination, mitigation, resolution,* and *follow-up.*

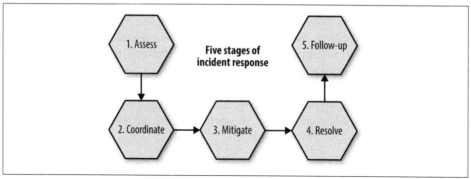

Figure 5-1. The five stages of incident response

Assessment

Whenever an alert is triggered by a change in a service's key metric (see Chapter 6, *Monitoring,* for more details on alerting, key metrics, and on-call rotations), and the developer on call for the service needs to respond to the alert, the very first step that needs to be taken is to *assess* the incident. The on-call engineer is the first responder, triaging every problem as soon as it triggers an alert, and his job is to determine the severity and scope of the issue.

Coordination

Once the incident has been assessed and triaged, the next step is to first *coordinate* with other developers and teams and then begin *communicating about the incident.* Very few developers on call for any given service will be able to resolve every single problem with the service, and so coordination with other teams who *can* resolve the issue will ensure that the problem is mitigated and resolved quickly. This means that there need to be clear channels of communication for incidents and outages so that any high-severity, high-scope problem can receive the immediate attention that it requires.

During the incident or outage, it's important to have a clear record of communication regarding the incident for several reasons. First, recording communication during the incident (in chat logs, over email, etc.) helps in diagnosing, root-causing, and mitigating the incident: everyone knows who is working on which fix, everyone knows what possible failures have been eliminated as possible causes, and once the root has been identified, everyone knows exactly what caused the problem. Second, other services that depend on the service experiencing the incident or outage need to be apprised of any problems so that they can mitigate its negative effects and ensure that their own service is protected from the failure. This keeps overall availability high, and prevents one service from bringing down entire dependency chains. Third, it helps when post-mortems are written for severe, global incidents by giving a clear, detailed record of exactly what happened and how the problem was triaged, mitigated, and resolved.

Mitigation

The third step is *mitigation*. After the problem has been assessed and organizational communication has begun (ensuring that the right people are working to fix the problem), developers need to work to reduce the impact of the incident on clients, the business, and anything else that may be affected by the incident. Mitigation is not the same as resolution: it is not *fixing* the root cause of the problem completely, only *reducing its impact*. An issue is not mitigated until both its availability and the availability of its clients are no longer compromised or suffering.

Resolution

After the effects of the incident or outage have been mitigated, engineers can work to *resolve* the root cause of the problem. This is the fourth step of the incident response process. This entails actually fixing the root cause of the problem, which may not have been done when the problem was mitigated. Most importantly, this is when the clock stops ticking. The two most important quantities that count against a microservice's SLA are time to detection (TTD) and time to mitigation (TTM). Once a problem has been mitigated, it should no longer be affecting end users or compromising the service's SLA, and so time to resolution (TTR) rarely (if ever) counts against a service's availability.

Follow-up

Three things need to happen in the fifth and final *follow-up* stage of incident response: postmortems need to be written to analyze and understand the incident or outage, severe incidents and outages need to be shared and reviewed, and a list of action items needs to be put together so that the development team(s) can complete them in order for the affected microservice(s) to return to a production-ready state (action items can often be fit into postmortems).

The most important aspect of incident follow-up is the *postmortem*. In general, a postmortem is a detailed document that follows every single incident and/or outage and contains critical information about what happened, why it happened, and what could have been done to prevent it. Every postmortem should, at the very minimum, contain a summary of what happened, data about what happened (time to detection, time to mitigation, time to resolution, total downtime, number of affected users, any relevant graphs and charts, etc.), a detailed timeline, a comprehensive root-cause analysis, a summary of how the incident could have been prevented, ways that similar outages can be prevented in the future, and a list of action items that need to be completed in order to bring the service back to a production-ready state. Postmortems are most effective when they're blameless, when they don't name names but only point out objective facts about the service. Pointing fingers, naming names, and blaming developers and engineers for outages stifles the organizational learning and sharing that is essential for maintaining a reliable, sustainable ecosystem.

Within large and complex microservice ecosystems, any failure or problem that brings one microservice down—whether big or small—almost certainly can (and will) affect at least one other microservice within the ecosystem. Communicating severe incidents and outages across various teams (and across the whole organization) can help catch these failures in other services before they occur. I've seen how effective incidents and outage reviews can be when done properly, and have watched developers attend these meetings and then rush off to their microservice afterward to fix any bugs in their own service that led to the incidents and/or outages that were reviewed.

Evaluate Your Microservice

Now that you have a better understanding of fault tolerance and catastrophe-preparedness, use the following list of questions to assess the production-readiness of your microservice(s) and microservice ecosystem. The questions are organized by topic, and correspond to the sections within this chapter.

Avoiding Single Points of Failure

- Does the microservice have a single point of failure?
- Does it have more than one point of failure?
- Can any points of failure be architected away, or do they need to be mitigated?

Catastrophes and Failure Scenarios

- Have all of the microservice's failure scenarios and possible catastrophes been identified?
- What are common failures across the microservice ecosystem?
- What are the hardware-layer failure scenarios that can affect this microservice?
- What communication-layer and application-layer failures can affect this microservice?
- What sorts of dependency failures can affect this microservice?
- What are the internal failures that could bring down this microservice?

Resiliency Testing

- Does this microservice have appropriate lint, unit, integration, and end-to-end tests?
- Does this microservice undergo regular, scheduled load testing?
- Are all possible failure scenarios implemented and tested using chaos testing?

Failure Detection and Remediation

- Are there standardized processes across the engineering organization(s) for handling incidents and outages?
- How do failures and outages of this microservice impact the business?
- Are there clearly defined levels of failure?
- Are there clearly defined mitigation strategies?
- Does the team follow the five stages of incident response when incidents and outages occur?

CHAPTER 6

Monitoring

A production-ready microservice is one that is properly monitored. Proper monitoring is one of the most important parts of building a production-ready microservice and guarantees higher microservice availability. In this chapter, the essential components of microservice monitoring are covered, including which key metrics to monitor, how to log key metrics, building dashboards that display key metrics, how to approach alerting, and on-call best practices.

Principles of Microservice Monitoring

The majority of outages in a microservice ecosystem are caused by bad deployments. The second most common cause of outages is the lack of proper *monitoring*. It's easy to see why this is the case. If the state of a microservice is unknown, if key metrics aren't tracked, then any precipitating failures will remain unknown until an actual outage occurs. By the time a microservice experiences an outage due to lack of monitoring, its availability has already been compromised. During these outages, the time to mitigation and time to repair are prolonged, pulling the availability of the microservice down even further: without easily accessible information about the microservice's key metrics, developers are often faced with a blank slate, unprepared to quickly resolve the issue. This is why proper monitoring is essential: it provides the development team with all of the relevant information about the microservice. When a microservice is properly monitored, its state is never unknown.

Monitoring a production-ready microservice has four components. The first is proper *logging* of all relevant and important information, which allows developers to understand the state of the microservice at any time in the present or in the past. The second is the use of well-designed *dashboards* that accurately reflect the health of the microservice, and are organized in such a way that anyone at the company could view the dashboard and understand the health and status of the microservice without difficulty. The third component is actionable and effective *alerting* on all key metrics, a practice that makes it easy for developers to mitigate and resolve problems with the microservice before they cause outages. The final component is the implementation and practice of running a sustainable *on-call rotation* responsible for the monitoring of the microservice. With effective logging, dashboards, alerting, and on-call rotation, the microservice's availability can be protected: failures and errors will be detected, mitigated, and resolved before they bring down any part of the microservice ecosystem.

A Production-Ready Service Is Properly Monitored

- Its key metrics are identified and monitored at the host, infrastructure, and microservice levels.
- It has appropriate logging that accurately reflects the past states of the microservice.
- Its dashboards are easy to interpret, and contain all key metrics.
- Its alerts are actionable and are defined by signal-providing thresholds.
- There is a dedicated on-call rotation responsible for monitoring and responding to any incidents and outages.
- There is a clear, well-defined, and standardized on-call procedure in place for handling incidents and outages.

Key Metrics

Before we jump into the components of proper monitoring, it's important to identify precisely *what* we want and need to monitor: we want to monitor a microservice, but what does that *actually* mean? A microservice isn't an individual object that we can follow or track, it cannot be isolated and quarantined—it's far more complicated than that. Deployed across dozens, if not hundreds, of servers, the behavior of a microservice is the sum of its behavior across all of its instantiations, which isn't the easiest thing to quantify. The key is identifying which properties of a microservice are necessary and sufficient for describing its behavior, and then determining what changes in those properties tell us about the overall status and health of the microservice. We'll call these properties *key metrics*.

There are two types of key metrics: host and infrastructure metrics, and microservice metrics. Host and infrastructure metrics are those that pertain to the status of the infrastructure and the servers on which the microservice is running, while microservice metrics are metrics that are unique to the individual microservice. In terms of the four-layer model of the microservice ecosystem as described in Chapter 1, *Micro-*

services, host and infrastructure metrics are metrics belonging to layers 1–3, while microservice metrics are those belonging to layer 4.

Separating key metrics into these two different types is important both organizationally and technically. Host and infrastructure metrics often affect more than one microservice: for example, if there is a problem with a particular server, and the microservice ecosystem shares the hardware resources among multiple microservices, host-level key metrics will be relevant to every microservice team that has a microservice deployed to that host. Likewise, microservice-specific metrics will rarely be applicable or useful to anyone but the team of developers working on that particular microservice. Teams should monitor both types of key metrics (that is, all metrics relevant to their microservice), and any metrics relevant to multiple microservices should be monitored and shared between the appropriate teams.

The host and infrastructure metrics that should be monitored for each microservice are the CPU utilized by the microservice on each host, the RAM utilized by the microservice on each host, the available threads, the microservice's open file descriptors (FD), and the number of database connections that the microservice has to any databases it uses. Monitoring these key metrics should be done in such a way that the status of each metric is accompanied by information about the infrastructure and the microservice. This means that monitoring should be granular enough that developers can know the status of the keys metrics for their microservice on any particular host and across all of the hosts that it runs on. For example, developers should be able to know how much CPU their microservice is using on one particular host *and* how much CPU their microservice is using across all hosts it runs on.

Monitoring Host-Level Metrics When Resources Are Abstracted

Some microservice ecosystems may use cluster management applications (like Mesos) in which the resources (CPU, RAM, etc.) are abstracted away from the host level. Host-level metrics won't be available in the same way to developers in these situations, but all key metrics for the microservice overall should still be monitored by the microservice team.

Determining the necessary and sufficient key metrics at the microservice level is a bit more complicated because it can depend on the particular language that the microservice is written in. Each language comes with its own special way of processing tasks, for example, and these language-specific features must be monitored closely in the majority of cases. Consider a Python service that utilizes uwsgi workers: the number of uwsgi workers is a necessary key metric for proper monitoring.

In addition to language-specific key metrics, we also must monitor the availability of the service, the service-level agreement (SLA) of the service, latency (of both the service as a whole and its API endpoints), success of API endpoints, responses and average response times of API endpoints, the services (clients) from which API requests originate (along with which endpoints they send requests to), errors and exceptions (both handled and unhandled), and the health and status of dependencies.

Importantly, all key metrics should be monitored everywhere that the application is deployed. This means that every stage of the deployment pipeline should be monitored. Staging must be closely monitored in order to catch any problems before a new candidate for production (a new build) is deployed to servers running production traffic. It almost goes without saying that all deployments to production servers should be monitored carefully, both in the canary and production deployment phases. (For more information on deployment pipelines, see Chapter 3, *Stability and Reliability*.)

Once the key metrics for a microservice have been identified, the next step is to capture the metrics emitted by your service. Capture them, and then log them, graph them, and alert on them. We'll cover each of these steps in the following sections.

Summary of Key Metrics

Host and infrastructure key metrics:

- CPU
- RAM
- Threads
- File descriptors
- Database connections

Microservice key metrics:

- Language-specific metrics
- Availability
- SLA
- Latency
- Endpoint success
- Endpoint responses
- Endpoint response times
- Clients
- Errors and exceptions
- Dependencies

Logging

Logging is the first component of production-ready monitoring. It begins and belongs in the codebase of each microservice, nestled deep within the code of each service, capturing all of the information necessary to describe the state of the microservice. In fact, describing the state of the microservice at any given time in the recent past is the ultimate goal of logging.

One of the benefits of microservice architecture is the freedom it gives developers to deploy new features and code changes frequently, and one of the consequences of this newfound developer freedom and increased development velocity is that the microservice is always changing. In most cases, the service will not be the same service it was 12 hours ago, let alone several days ago, and reproducing any problems will be impossible. When faced with a problem, often the only way to determine the root cause of an incident or outage is to comb through the logs, discover the state of the microservice at the time of the outage, and figure out why the service failed in that state. Logging needs to be such that developers can determine from the logs exactly what went wrong and where things fell apart.

Logging Without Microservice Versioning

Microservice versioning is often discouraged because it can lead to other (client) services pinning to specific versions of a microservice that may not be the best or most updated version of the microservice. Without versioning, determining the state of a microservice when a failure or outage occurred can be difficult, but thorough logging can prevent this from becoming a problem: if the logging is good enough that state of a microservice at the *time* of an outage can be sufficiently known and understood, the lack of versioning ceases to be a hindrance to quick and effective mitigation and resolution.

Determining precisely *what* to log is specific to each microservice. The best guidance on determining what needs to be logged is, somewhat unfortunately, necessarily vague: log whatever information is essential to describing the state of the service at a given time. Luckily, we can narrow down which information is necessary by restricting our logging to whatever can be contained in the code of the service. Host-level and infrastructure-level information won't (and shouldn't) be logged by the application itself, but by services and tools running the application platform. Some microservice-level key metrics and information, like hashed user IDs and request and response details can and should be located in the microservice's logs.

There are, of course, some things that *should never, ever be logged*. Logs should never contain identifying information, such as names of customers, Social Security numbers, and other private data. They should never contain information that could present a security risk, such as passwords, access keys, or secrets. In most cases, even seemingly innocuous things like user IDs and usernames should not be logged unless encrypted.

At times, logging at the individual microservice level will not be enough. As we've seen throughout this book, microservices do not live alone, but within complex chains of clients and dependencies within the microservice ecosystem. While developers can try their best to log and monitor everything important and relevant to their service, tracking and logging requests and responses throughout the entire client and dependency chains from end-to-end can illuminate important information about the system that would otherwise go unknown (such as total latency and availability of the stack). To make this information accessible and visible, building a production-ready microservice ecosystem requires tracing each request through the entire stack.

The reader might have noticed at this point that it appears that a lot of information needs to be logged. Logs are data, and logging is expensive: they are expensive to store, they are expensive to access, and both storing and accessing logs comes with the additional cost associated with making expensive calls over the network. The cost of storing logs may not seem like much for an individual microservice, but if the logging needs of all the microservices within a microservice ecosystem are added together, the cost is rather high.

Logs and Debugging

Avoid adding debugging logs in code that will be deployed to production—such logs are very costly. If any logs are added specifically for the purpose of debugging, developers should take great care to ensure that any branch or build containing these additional logs does not ever touch production.

Logging needs to be scalable, it needs to be available, and it needs to be easily accessible *and* searchable. To keep the cost of logs down and to ensure scalability and high availability, it's often necessary to impose per-service logging quotas along with limits and standards on what information can be logged, how many logs each microservice can store, and how long the logs will be stored before being deleted.

Dashboards

Every microservice must have at least one *dashboard* where all key metrics (such as hardware utilization, database connections, availability, latency, responses, and the status of API endpoints) are collected and displayed. A dashboard is a graphical display that is updated in real time to reflect all the most important information about a microservice. Dashboards should be easily accessible, centralized, and standardized across the microservice ecosystem.

Dashboards should be easy to interpret so that an outsider can quickly determine the health of the microservice: anyone should be able to look at the dashboard and know immediately whether or not the microservice is working correctly. This requires striking a balance between overloading a viewer with information (which would render the dashboard effectively useless) and not displaying enough information (which would also make the dashboard useless): only the necessary minimum of information about key metrics should be displayed.

A dashboard should also serve as an accurate reflection of the overall quality of monitoring of the entire microservice. Any key metric that is alerted on should be included in the dashboard (we will cover this in the next section): the exclusion of any key metric in the dashboard will reflect poor monitoring of the service, while the inclusion of metrics that are not necessary will reflect a neglect of alerting (and, consequently, monitoring) best practices.

There are several exceptions to the rule against inclusion of nonkey metrics. In addition to key metrics, information about each phase of the deployment pipeline should be displayed, though not necessarily within the same dashboard. Developers working on microservices that require monitoring a large number of key metrics may opt to set up separate dashboards for each deployment phase (one for staging, one for canary, and one for production) to accurately reflect the health of the microservice at each deployment phase: since different builds will be running on the deployment phases simultaneously, accurately reflecting the health of the microservice in a dashboard might require approaching dashboard design with the goal of reflecting the health of the microservice at a particular deployment phase (treating them almost as different microservices, or at least as different instantiations of a microservice).

Dashboards and Outage Detection

Even though dashboards can illuminate anomalies and negative trends of a microservice's key metrics, developers should never need to watch a microservice's dashboard in order to detect incidents and outages. Doing so is an anti-pattern that leads to deficiencies in alerting and overall monitoring.

To assist in determining problems introduced by new deployments, it helps to include information about when a deployment occurred in the dashboard. The most effective and useful way to accomplish this is to make sure that deployment times are shown within the graphs of each key metric. Doing so allows developers to quickly check graphs after each deployment to see if any strange patterns emerge in any of the key metrics.

Well-designed dashboards also give developers an easy, visual way to detect anomalies and determine alerting thresholds. Very slight or gradual changes or disturbances in key metrics run the risk of not being caught by alerting, but a careful look at an accurate dashboard can illuminate anomalies that would otherwise go undetected. Alerting thresholds, which we will cover in the next section, are notoriously difficult to determine, but can be set appropriately when historical data on the dashboard is examined: developers can see normal patterns in key metrics, view spikes in metrics that occurred with outages (or led to outages) in the past, and then set thresholds accordingly.

Alerting

The third component of monitoring a production-ready microservice is real-time *alerting*. The detection of failures, as well as the detection of changes within key metrics that could lead to a failure, is accomplished through alerting. To ensure this, all key metrics—host-level metrics, infrastructure metrics, and microservice-specific metrics—should be alerted on, with alerts set at various thresholds. Effective and actionable alerting is essential to preserving the availability of a microservice and preventing downtime.

Setting up Effective Alerting

Alerts must be set up for all key metrics. Any change in a key metric at the host level, infrastructure level, or microservice level that could lead to an outage, cause a spike in latency, or somehow harm the availability of the microservice should trigger an alert. Importantly, alerts should also be triggered whenever a key metric is *not* seen.

All alerts should be useful: they should be defined by good, signal-providing thresholds. Three types of thresholds should be set for each key metric, and have both upper and lower bounds: *normal*, *warning*, and *critical*. Normal thresholds reflect the usual, appropriate upper and lower bounds of each key metric and shouldn't ever trigger an alert. Warning thresholds on each key metric will trigger alerts when there is a deviation from the norm that could lead to a problem with the microservice; warning thresholds should be set such that they will trigger alerts *before* any deviations from the norm cause an outage or otherwise negatively affect the microservice. Critical thresholds should be set based on which upper and lower bounds on key metrics actually cause an outage, cause latency to spike, or otherwise hurt a microservice's availability. In an ideal world, warning thresholds should trigger alerts that lead to quick detection, mitigation, and resolution before any critical thresholds are reached. In each category, thresholds should be high enough to avoid noise, but low enough to catch any and all real problems with key metrics.

Determining Thresholds Early in the Lifecycle of a Microservice

Thresholds for key metrics can be very difficult to set without historical data. Any thresholds set early in a microservice's lifecycle run the risk of either being useless or triggering too many alerts. To determine the appropriate thresholds for a new microservice (or even an old one), developers can run load testing on the microservice to gauge where the thresholds should lie. Running "normal" traffic loads through the microservice can determine the normal thresholds, while running larger-than-expected traffic loads can help determine warning and critical thresholds.

All alerts need to be actionable. Nonactionable alerts are those that are triggered and then resolved (or ignored) by the developer(s) on call for the microservice because they are not important, not relevant, do not signify that anything is wrong with the microservice, or alert on a problem that cannot be resolved by the developer(s). Any alert that cannot be immediately acted on by the on-call developer(s) should be removed from the pool of alerts, reassigned to the relevant on-call rotation, or (if possible) changed so that it becomes actionable.

Some of the key microservice metrics run the risk of being nonactionable. For example, alerting on the availability of dependencies can easily lead to nonactionable alerts if dependency outages, increases in dependency latency, or dependency downtime do not require any action to be taken by their client(s). If no action needs to be taken, then the thresholds should be set appropriately, or in more extreme cases, no alerts should be set on dependencies at all. However, if any action at all should be taken, even something as small as contacting the dependency's on-call or development team in order to alert them to the issue and/or coordinate mitigation and resolution, then an alert should be triggered.

Handling Alerts

Once an alert has been triggered, it needs to be handled quickly and effectively. The root cause of the triggered alert should be mitigated and resolved. To quickly and effectively handle alerts, there are several steps that can be taken.

The first step is to create step-by-step instructions for each known alert that detail how to triage, mitigate, and resolve each alert. These step-by-step alert instructions should live within an on-call runbook within the centralized documentation of each microservice, making them easily accessible to anyone who is on call for the microservice (more details on runbooks can be found in Chapter 7, *Documentation and Understanding*). Runbooks are crucial to the monitoring of a microservice: they allow any on-call developer to have step-by-step instructions on how to mitigate and resolve the root causes of each alert. Since each alert is tied to a deviation in a key metric, runbooks can be written so that they address each key metric, known causes of deviations from the norm, and how to go about debugging the problem.

Two types of on-call runbooks should be created. The first are runbooks for host-level and infrastructure-level alerts that should be shared between the whole engineering organization—these should be written for every key host-level and infrastructure-level metric. The second are on-call runbooks for specific microservices that have step-by-step instructions regarding microservice-specific alerts triggered by changes in key metrics; for example, a spike in latency should trigger an alert, and there should be step-by-step instructions in the on-call runbook that clearly document how to debug, mitigate, and resolve spikes in the microservice's latency.

The second step is to identify alerting anti-patterns. If the microservice on-call rotation is overwhelmed by alerts yet the microservice appears to work as expected, then any alerts that are seen more than once but that can be easily mitigated and/or resolved should be automated away. That is, build the mitigation and/or resolution steps into the microservice itself. This holds for every alert, and writing step-by-step instructions for alerts within on-call runbooks allows executing on this strategy to be rather effective. In fact, any alert that, once triggered, requires a simple set of steps to be taken in order to be mitigated and resolved, can be easily automated away. Once this level of production-ready monitoring has been established, a microservice should never experience the same exact problem twice.

On-Call Rotations

In a microservice ecosystem, the development teams themselves are responsible for the availability of their microservices. Where monitoring is concerned, this means that developers need to be on call for their own microservices. The goal of each developer on-call for a microservice needs to be clear: they are to detect, mitigate, and resolve any issue that arises with the microservice during their on call shift before the issue causes an outage for their microservice or impacts the business itself.

In some larger engineering organizations, site reliability engineers, DevOps, or other operations engineers may take on the responsibility for monitoring and on call, but this requires each microservice to be relatively stable and reliable before the on-call responsibilities can be handed off to another team. In most microservice ecosystems, microservices rarely reach this high level of stability because, as we've seen throughout the previous chapters, microservices are constantly changing. In a microservice ecosystem, developers need to bear the responsibility of monitoring the code that they deploy.

Designing good on-call rotations is crucial and requires the involvement of the entire team. To prevent burnout, on-call rotations should be both brief and shared: no fewer than two developers should ever be on call at one time, and on-call shifts should last no longer than one week and be spaced no more frequently than one month apart.

The on-call rotations of each microservice should be internally publicized and easily accessible. If a microservice team is experiencing issues with one of their dependencies, they should be able to track down the on-call engineers for the microservice and contact them very quickly. Hosting this information in a centralized place helps to make developers more effective in triaging problems and preventing outages.

Developing standardized on-call procedures across an engineering organization will go a long way toward building a sustainable microservice ecosystem. Developers should be trained about how to approach their on-call shifts, be made aware of on-call best practices, and be ramped up for joining the on-call rotation very quickly. Standardizing this process and making on-call expectations completely clear to every developer will prevent the burnout, confusion, and frustration that usually accompanies any mention of joining an on-call rotation.

Evaluate Your Microservice

Now that you have a better understanding of monitoring, use the following list of questions to assess the production-readiness of your microservice(s) and microservice ecosystem. The questions are organized by topic, and correspond to the sections within this chapter.

Key Metrics

- What are this microservice's key metrics?
- What are the host and infrastructure metrics?
- What are the microservice-level metrics?
- Are all the microservice's key metrics monitored?

Logging

- What information does this microservice need to log?
- Does this microservice log all important requests?
- Does the logging accurately reflect the state of the microservice at any given time?
- Is this logging solution cost-effective and scalable?

Dashboards

- Does this microservice have a dashboard?
- Is the dashboard easy to interpret? Are all key metrics displayed on the dashboard?
- Can I determine whether or not this microservice is working correctly by looking at the dashboard?

Alerting

- Is there an alert for every key metric?
- Are all alerts defined by good, signal-providing thresholds?
- Are alert thresholds set appropriately so that alerts will fire before an outage occurs?
- Are all alerts actionable?
- Are there step-by-step triage, mitigation, and resolution instructions for each alert in the on-call runbook?

On-Call Rotations

- Is there a dedicated on-call rotation responsible for monitoring this microservice?
- Is there a minimum of two developers on each on-call shift?
- Are there standardized on-call procedures across the engineering organization?

CHAPTER 7

Documentation and Understanding

A production-ready microservice is documented and understood. Documentation and organizational understanding increase developer velocity while mitigating two of the most significant trade-offs that come with the adoption of microservice architecture: organizational sprawl and technical debt. This chapter explores the essential elements of documenting and understanding a microservice, including how to build comprehensive and useful documentation, how to increase microservice understanding at every level of the microservice ecosystem, and how to implement production-readiness throughout an engineering organization.

Principles of Microservice Documentation and Understanding

I'm going to open this final chapter on the last principle of microservice standardization with a famous story from Russian literature. While it may seem rather unorthodox to quote Dostoyevsky in a book on software architecture, the character Grushenka in *The Brothers Karamazov* captures so perfectly what I believe to be the key of microservice documentation and understanding: "Just know one thing, Rakitka, I may be wicked, but still I gave an onion."

My favorite part of Dostoyevsky's brilliant novel is a tale told by the character Grushenka about an old woman and an onion. The tale goes something like this: there was once an old, bitter woman who was very selfish and heartless. One day, she happened upon a beggar, and for some reason, felt a great deal of pity. She wanted to give something to the beggar, but all she had was an onion, so she gave her onion to the beggar. The old woman eventually died, and thanks to her bitterness and coldness of heart, ended up in hell. After she had suffered for quite some time, an angel came to save her, for God had remembered her one selfless deed in life, and wanted to extend the same kindness in return. The angel reached out to her with an onion in his hand. The old woman grabbed the onion, but to her dismay, the other sinners around her reached for the onion too. Her cold, bitter nature kicked in, and she tried to fight them off, not wanting any of them to have any piece of the onion, and sadly, as she tried to claw the onion away from them, the onion split into many layers and she and the other sinners fell back into hell.

It's not the most heartwarming tale, but there's a moral to Grushenka's story that I have found remarkably applicable to the practice of microservice documentation: always give an onion.

The importance of thorough, updated documentation for every microservice cannot be emphasized enough. Ask developers working in a microservice ecosystem what their main concerns are, and they'll rattle off a list of features still to be implemented, bugs to be fixed, dependencies that are causing trouble, and things that they don't understand about their own service and the dependencies they rely on. When asked to go into greater detail about the latter two things, they tend to give similar answers: they don't understand how it works, it's a black box, and the documentation is completely useless.

Poor documentation of dependencies and internal tools slows developers down and affects their ability to make their own services production-ready. It prevents them from using dependencies and internal tools correctly and wastes countless engineering hours, because sometimes the only way to figure out what a service or tool does (without proper documentation) is to reverse-engineer it until you understand how it works.

Poor documentation of a service also hurts the productivity of the developers who are contributing to it. For example, the lack of runbooks for an on-call shift means whoever is on call will need to figure out each problem from square one every single time. Without an onboarding guide, each new developer working on the service will need to start from scratch to understand how the service works. Single points of failure and problems with the service will go unnoticed until they cause an outage. New features added to the service will often miss the big picture of how the service actually works.

The goal of good, production-ready documentation is to create and maintain a centralized repository of knowledge about the service. Sharing that knowledge has two components: the bare facts about the service, and organizational understanding of what the service does and where it fits into the organization as a whole. The problem of poor documentation can then be divided into two subproblems: lack of documentation (the facts) and lack of understanding. Solving these two subproblems requires standardizing documentation for every microservice and putting organizational structures into place for sharing microservice understanding.

Grushenka's tale is the golden rule of microservice documentation: always give an onion. Give an onion for your sake, for the sake of fellow developers working on your service, and for the sake of the developers whose services depend on yours.

A Production-Ready Service Is Documented and Understood

- It has comprehensive documentation.
- Its documentation is updated regularly.
- Its documentation contains a description of the microservice; an architecture diagram; contact and on-call information; links to important information; an onboarding and development guide; information about the service's request flow(s), endpoints, and dependencies; an on-call runbook; and answers to frequently asked questions.
- It is well understood at the developer, team, and organizational levels.
- It is held to a set of production-readiness standards and meets the associated requirements.
- Its architecture is reviewed and audited frequently.

Microservice Documentation

The documentation for all microservices in an engineering organization should be stored in a centralized, shared, and easily accessible place. Any developer on any team should be able to find the documentation for every microservice without any difficulty. An internal website containing the documentation for all microservices and internal tools tends to be the best medium for this.

READMEs and Code Comments Are Not Documentation

Many developers limit the documentation of their microservices to a README file in their repository or to comments scattered throughout the code. While having a README is essential, and all microservice code should contain appropriate comments, this is *not* production-ready documentation and requires that developers check out and search through the code. Proper documentation is stored in a centralized place (like a website) where the documentation for all microservices in the engineering organization lives.

The documentation should be updated regularly. Any time a significant change is made to the service, the documentation should be updated. For example, if a new API endpoint is added, information about the endpoint must be added to the documentation as well. If a new alert is added, then step-by-step instructions on how to triage, mitigate, and resolve the alert should also be added to the service's on-call runbook. If a new dependency is added, then information about that dependency should be added to the documentation. Always give an onion.

The best way to accomplish this is to make the process of updating documentation part of the development workflow. If updating documentation is seen as a separate task aside from (and secondary to) development, then it will never get done and will become part of the technical debt of the service. To reduce technical debt, developers should be encouraged (or, if need be, required) to accompany every significant code change with an update to the documentation.

Make Updating Documentation Part of the Development Cycle

If updating and improving documentation is viewed as secondary to writing code, it will often be pushed off and become part of the technical debt of the service. To avoid this, make documentation updates and improvements a required part of the development cycle of the service.

Documentation should be both comprehensive and useful. It should contain all of the relevant and important facts about the service. After reading through the documentation, a developer should know how to develop and contribute to the service; the architecture of the service; the contact and on-call information for the service; how the service works (request flows, endpoints, dependencies, etc.); how to triage, mitigate, and fix incidents and outages as well as resolve alerts generated by the service; and answers to frequently asked questions about the service.

Most importantly, documentation should be written clearly and should be easy to understand. Jargon-heavy documentation is useless, documentation that is overly technical and doesn't explain things that may be unique to the service is also useless, as is documentation that doesn't go into any significant detail at all. The goal in writing good, clean, and clear documentation is to write it so that it can be understood by any developer, manager, product manager, or executive within the company.

Let's dive a little bit deeper into each of the elements of production-ready microservice documentation.

Description

Each microservice's documentation should begin with a *description* of the service. It should be short, sweet, and to the point. For example, if there is a microservice called *receipt-sender* whose purpose is to send a receipt after a customer completes an order, the description should read:

Description:

After a customer places an order, receipt-sender sends a receipt to the customer via email.

This is essential because it ensures that anyone who finds the documentation will know what role the microservice plays in the microservice ecosystem.

Architecture Diagram

The description of the service should be followed by an *architecture diagram*. This diagram should detail the architecture of the service, including its components, its endpoints, the request flow, its dependencies (both upstream and downstream), and information about any databases or caches. See an example architecture diagram in Figure 7-1.

Architecture diagrams are essential for several reasons. It's nearly impossible to understand how and why a microservice works just by reading through the code, and so a well-designed architecture diagram is an easily understandable visual description and summary of the microservice. These diagrams also aid developers in adding new features by abstracting away the inner workings of the service so that developers can see where and how new features will (or will not) fit. Most importantly, they illuminate issues and problems with the service that would go unnoticed without a complete visual representation of its architecture: it's difficult to discover a service's points of failure by combing through lines of code, but they tend to stick out like sore thumbs in an accurate architecture diagram.

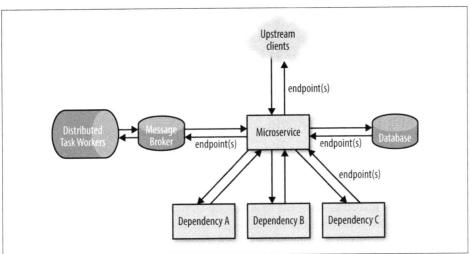

Figure 7-1. Example microservice architecture diagram

Contact and On-Call Information

Chances are, anyone looking at a service's documentation will either be someone on the service team, or someone on a different team who is experiencing trouble with the service or wants to know how the service works. For developers in the second group, having access to information about the team is both useful and necessary, and so several important facts should be included in a *contact and on-call information* section within the documentation.

This section should include the names, positions, and contact information of everyone on the team (including individual contributors, managers, and program/product managers). This makes it easy for developers on other teams to quickly determine who they should contact if they experience a problem with the service or have a question about it. This information is useful, for example, when a developer is experiencing problems with one of their dependencies: knowing who to contact and what their role is on the team makes cross-team communication easy and efficient.

Adding information about the on-call rotation (and keeping it updated so that it reflects who is on call for the service at any given time) will ensure that people will know exactly who to contact for general problems or emergencies: the engineer who is on call for the service.

Links

Documentation needs to be a centralized resource for all the information about a microservice. In order for this to be true, the documentation needs to contain links to the repository (so that developers can easily check out the code), a link to the dashboard, a link to the original RFC for the microservice, and a link to the most recent architecture review slides. Any extra information about other microservices, technologies used by the microservice, etc., that may be useful to the developer should be included in a *links* section of the documentation.

Onboarding and Development Guide

The purpose of an *onboarding and development* section is to make it easy for a new developer to onboard to the team, begin contributing code, add features to the microservice, and introduce new changes into the deployment pipeline.

The first part of this section should be a step-by-step guide to setting up the service. It should walk a developer through checking out the code, setting up the environment, starting the service, and verifying that the service is working correctly (including all commands or scripts that need to be run in order to accomplish this).

The second part should guide the developer through the development cycle and deployment pipeline of the service (details of a production-ready development cycle and deployment pipeline can be found in "The Development Cycle" on page 42 and "The Deployment Pipeline" on page 44). This should include the technical details (e.g., commands that must be run, along with several examples) of each of the steps: how to check out the code, how to make a change to the code, how to write a unit test for the change (if necessary), how to run the required tests, how to commit their changes, how to send changes for code review, how to make sure that the service is built and released correctly, and then how to deploy (as well as how the deployment pipeline is set up for the service).

Request Flows, Endpoints, and Dependencies

The documentation should also contain critical information about *request flows, endpoints, and dependencies* of the microservice.

Request flow documentation can consist of a diagram of the request flows of the application. This can be the architecture diagram, if the request flow is detailed appropriately within the architecture diagram. Any diagram should be accompanied by a qualitative description of the types of requests that are made to the microservice and how they are handled.

This is also the place to document all API endpoints of the service. A bulleted list of the endpoints with their names and a qualitative description of each along with their responses is usually sufficient. It must be clear and understandable enough that another developer working on a different team could read the descriptions of your service's API endpoints and treat your microservice as a black box, hitting the endpoints successfully and receiving the expected responses.

The third element of this section is information about the service's dependencies. List the dependencies, the relevant endpoints of these dependencies, and any requests the service makes to them, along with information about their SLAs, any alternatives/caching/backups in place in case of failure, and links to their documentation and dashboards.

On-Call Runbooks

As covered in Chapter 6, *Monitoring*, every single alert should be included in an on-call runbook and accompanied by step-by-step instructions describing how it should be triaged, mitigated, and resolved. The on-call runbook should be kept in the centralized documentation of the service, in an *on-call runbook* section, along with both general and detailed guidance on troubleshooting and debugging new errors.

A good runbook will begin with any general on-call requirements and procedures, and then contain a complete list of the service's alerts. For each alert, the on-call runbook should include the alert name, a description of the alert, a description of the problem, and a step-by-step guide on how to triage the alert, mitigate it, and then resolve it. It will also describe any organizational implications of the alert: the severity of the problem, whether or not the alert signifies an outage, and information about how to communicate any incidents and outages to the team, and if necessary, to the rest of the engineering organization.

Write On-Call Runbooks That Sleepy Developers Can Understand at 2 A.M.

Developers on call for a service may (or, more realistically, will) be paged at any hour of the day, including late at night or very early in the morning. Write your on-call runbooks so that a half-asleep developer will be able to follow along without any difficulty.

Writing good, clear, easily understandable on-call runbooks is extremely important. They should be written so that any developer who is on call for the service or who is experiencing trouble with the service will be able to act quickly, diagnose the problem, mitigate the incident, and resolve, all in an extremely small amount of time in order to keep the downtime of the service very, very low.

Not every alert will be easily mitigated or resolved, and most outages (aside from those caused by code bugs introduced by a recent deployment) haven't been seen before. To equip developers to handle these problems wisely, add a general *troubleshooting and debugging* section to the on-call runbook in the documentation that is filled with tips on how to approach new problems in a strategic and methodical way.

FAQ

An often forgotten element of documentation is a section devoted to answering common questions about the service. Having a "Frequently Asked Questions" section takes the burden of answering common questions off of whomever is on call and, consequently, the rest of the team.

There are two categories of questions that should be answered here. The first are questions that developers on other teams ask about the service. The way to approach answering these questions in an FAQ setting is simple: if someone asks you a question, and you think it might be asked again, add it to the FAQ. The second category of questions are those that come from team members, and the same approach can be taken here: if there's a question about how or why or when to do something related to the service, add it to the FAQ.

Summary: Elements of Production-Ready Microservice Documentation

Production-ready microservice documentation includes:

- A description of the microservice and its place in the overall microservice ecosystem and the business

- An architecture diagram detailing the architecture of the service and its clients and dependencies at a high level of abstraction

- Contact and on-call information about the microservice's development team

- Links to the repository, dashboard(s), the RFC for the service, architecture reviews, and any other relevant or useful information

- An onboarding and development guide containing details about the development process, the deployment pipeline, and any other information that will be useful to developers who contribute code to the service

- Detailed information about the microservice's request flows, SLA, production-readiness status, API endpoints, important clients, and dependencies

- An on-call runbook containing general incident and outage response procedures, step-by-step instructions on how to triage, mitigate, and resolve each alert, and a general troubleshooting and debugging section

- A "Frequently Asked Questions" (FAQ) section

Microservice Understanding

Centralized, updated, and thorough documentation is only one part of production-ready microservice documentation and understanding. Aside from writing and updating documentation, organizational processes should be put into place to ensure that microservices are well understood not only by the individual development teams but by the organization as a whole. In many ways, a well-understood microservice is one that meets every production-readiness requirement.

Microservice understanding is truly indispensable to the developer, the team, and the organization. While the notion of "understanding" a microservice may seem too vague to be useful at first glance, the concept of a production-ready microservice can be used to guide and define microservice understanding at every level. Armed with production-readiness standards and requirements, along with a realistic understanding of organizational complexity and the challenges that microservice architecture brings to the arena, developers can quantify their understanding of each microservice and (as I've urged the reader earlier in this chapter) can give an onion to the rest of the organization.

For the individual developer, this translates to being able to answer questions about her microservice. For example, when asked if her microservice is scalable, she will be able to look at a list of scalability requirements and confidently answer "Yes," "No," or something in between (e.g., "It meets requirements x and z, but y has not yet been implemented"). Likewise, when asked if her microservice is fault tolerant, she'll be able to rattle off all failure scenarios and possible catastrophes, then explain in detail how she has prepared for these using various types of resiliency testing.

At the team level, *understanding* signifies that the team is aware of where their microservice stands with regard to production-readiness and what needs to be accomplished to bring their service to a production-ready state. This has to be a cultural element of each team in order for it to be successful: production-readiness standards and requirements need to drive the decisions made by the team and be seen not merely as boxes to check off on a checklist, but rather as principles that guide the team toward building the best possible microservice.

Understanding needs to be built into the fabric of the organization itself. This requires that production-readiness standards and requirements become part of the organizational process. Before a service is even built, and a *request for comments* (RFC) is sent around for review, the service can be evaluated against the production-readiness standards and requirements. Developers, architects, and operations engineers can make sure that the service is built for stability, reliability, scalability, performance, fault tolerance, catastrophe-preparedness, proper monitoring, and appropriately documented and understood before it even begins running—ensuring that once the new service begins to host production traffic, it has been architected and optimized for availability and can be trusted with production traffic.

It's not enough to only review and architect for production-readiness at the beginning of a microservice's lifecycle. Existing services need to be reviewed and audited constantly so that the quality of each microservice is kept at a sufficiently high level, ensuring high availability and trust across various microservice teams and the entire microservice ecosystem. Automating these production-readiness audits of existing services and internally publicizing the results can help to establish awareness across the organization about the quality of the overall microservice ecosystem.

Architecture Reviews

One thing I've learned after driving these production-readiness standards and their requirements across over a thousand different microservices and their development teams is that the most immediately effective way to accomplish microservice understanding is to hold scheduled *architecture reviews* for each microservice. A good architecture review is a meeting where any and all developers and site reliability engineers (or other operations engineers) working on the service meet in a room, draw up the architecture of the service on a whiteboard, and thoroughly evaluate its architecture.

Within several minutes into this exercise, it tends to become very clear precisely what the scope of understanding is at the developer and team levels. Talking through the architecture, developers will quickly discover scalability and performance bottlenecks, previously undiscovered points of failure, possible outages and future incidents and failures and catastrophe scenarios, and new features that should be added. Poor architectural decisions that were made in the past will become obvious, and old technologies that should be replaced by newer and/or better ones will stand out. To ensure that evaluation and discussion is productive and objective, it's helpful to bring in developers from other teams (especially those in infrastructure, DevOps, or site reliability engineering) who have experience in large-scale distributed systems architecture (and the organization's specific microservice ecosystem) and will be able to point out problems that developers may not notice.

Each meeting should produce a new, updated architecture diagram for the service, along with a list of projects to tackle in the coming weeks and months. The new diagram should definitely be added to the documentation, and projects can be included in each service's *roadmap* (see "Production-Readiness Roadmaps" on page 128) and *objectives and key results* (OKRs).

Because microservice development moves rather quickly, microservices evolve at a rapid pace and the lower layers of the microservice ecosystem will be constantly changing. In order to keep the architecture and its understanding relevant and productive, these meetings should be held regularly. I've found that a good rule of thumb is to schedule them so that they align with OKR and project planning. If projects and OKRs are planned and scheduled quarterly, then quarterly architecture reviews should be held each quarter before the planning cycle begins.

Production-Readiness Audits

To make sure that a microservice meets production-readiness standards and requirements and is actually production-ready, the team can run a *production-readiness audit* on the service. Running an audit is quite simple: the team sits down with a checklist of the production-readiness requirements and checks off whether or not their service meets each requirement. This enables understanding of a service: each developer and team will know, by the end of the audit, exactly where their service stands and where things can be improved.

The structure of an audit should mirror the production-readiness standards and requirements that the engineering organization has adopted. The team should use the audits to quantify the stability, reliability, scalability, fault tolerance, catastrophe-preparedness, performance, monitoring, and documentation of the service. As I've described in earlier chapters, each of these standards is accompanied by a set of requirements that can be used to bring each service up to those standards—developers can adjust these requirements of each production-readiness standard so that they meet the needs and goals of the organization. The exact requirements will depend on the details of the company's microservice ecosystem, but the standards and their basic components are relevant across every ecosystem (see Appendix A for a summary checklist containing the production-readiness standards and their general requirements).

Production-Readiness Roadmaps

Once a microservice development team has completed a thorough production-readiness audit of their microservice and the team understands whether their service is production-ready, the next step is to plan how to bring the service to a production-ready state. Audits make this easy: at this point, the team has a checklist of which production-readiness requirements their service doesn't meet, and all that is left to do is to satisfy each unfulfilled requirement.

This is where *production-readiness roadmaps* can be developed, and I've found them to be an extremely useful piece of the production-readiness and microservice understanding process. Each microservice is different, and the implementation details of each unsatisfied requirement will vary between services, so producing a detailed roadmap that documents all of the implementation details will guide the team toward making their microservice production-ready. Requirements that need to be met can be accompanied by the technical details, problems that have arisen (outages and incidents) that are related to the requirement, a link to some ticket in a task-management system, and the name(s) of the developer(s) who will be working on the project.

The roadmap and the list of unsatisfied production-readiness requirements it contains can become part of whatever planning and (if used at the company) OKRs are in store for the service. Satisfying production-readiness requirements works best when the process goes hand in hand both with feature development and with the adoption of new technologies. Making each service in the microservice ecosystem stable, reliable, scalable, performant, fault tolerant, catastrophe-prepared, monitored, documented, and understood is a straightforward, quantifiable way to guarantee that each service is truly production-ready, ensuring the availability of the entire microservice ecosystem.

Production-Readiness Automation

Architecture reviews, audits, and roadmaps solve the challenges of microservice understanding at the developer and team levels, but understanding at an organizational level requires an additional component. As I've presented it so far, all of the work that goes into building a production-ready microservice is mostly manual, requiring developers to individually follow each audit step, make tasks and lists and roadmaps and check off individual requirement boxes. Manual work like this often gets put on the back burner to join the rest of the technical debt, even in the most productive and production-readiness driven teams.

One of the key principles of software engineering in practice is this: if you have to do something manually more than once, automate it so that you never have to do it again. This applies to operational work, it applies to any one-off, ad hoc situations and anything you need to type into a terminal, and not surprisingly, it applies to enforcing production-readiness standards across an engineering organization. Automation is the best onion you can give to your development teams.

It's easy to make a list of the production-readiness requirements for every microservice. I've done it myself at Uber, I've seen other developers implement the very same production-readiness standards in this book at their own companies, and I've created a template checklist (Appendix A, *Production-Readiness Checklist*) that you, the reader, can use. A list like this makes automating the checklist rather easy. For example, to check for fault tolerance and catastrophe-preparedness, you can run automated checks to ensure that the proper resiliency tests are in place, are running, and that each microservice passes the tests with flying colors.

The difficulty in automating each of these production-readiness checks will depend entirely on the complexity of your internal services within each layer of the microservice ecosystem. If all microservices and self-service tools have decent APIs, automation is a breeze. If your services have trouble communicating, or if any self-service internal tools are finicky or poorly written, you're going to have a bad time (and not just with production-readiness, but with the integrity of your service and the entire microservice ecosystem).

Automating production-readiness increases organizational understanding in several extremely important and effective ways. If you automate these checks and run them constantly, teams in the organization will always know where each microservice stands. Publicize these results internally, give each microservice a production-readiness score measuring how production-ready their service is, require business-critical services to have a high minimum production-readiness score, and gate deployments. Production-readiness can be made part of the engineering culture, and this is one surefire way you can accomplish that.

Evaluate Your Microservice

Now that you have a better understanding of documentation, use the following list of questions to assess the production-readiness of your microservice(s) and microservice ecosystem. The questions are organized by topic, and correspond to the sections within this chapter.

Microservice Documentation

- Is the documentation for all microservices stored in a centralized, shared, and easily accessible place?
- Is the documentation easily searchable?
- Are significant changes to the microservice accompanied by updates to the microservice's documentation?
- Does the microservice's documentation contain a description of the microservice?
- Does the microservice's documentation contain an architecture diagram?
- Does the microservice's documentation contain contact and on-call information?
- Does the microservice's documentation contain links to important information?
- Does the microservice's documentation contain an onboarding and development guide?
- Does the microservice's documentation contain information about the microservice's request flow, endpoints, and dependencies?
- Does the microservice's documentation contain an on-call runbook?
- Does the microservice's documentation contain an FAQ section?

Microservice Understanding

- Can every developer on the team answer questions about the production-readiness of the microservice?
- Is there a set of principles and standards that all microservices are held to?
- Is there an RFC process in place for every new microservice?
- Are existing microservices reviewed and audited frequently?
- Are architecture reviews held for every microservice team?
- Is there a production-readiness audit process in place?
- Are production-readiness roadmaps used to bring the microservice to a production-ready state?
- Do the production-readiness standards drive the organization's OKRs?
- Is the production-readiness process automated?

Production-Readiness Checklist

This will be a checklist to run over all microservices—manually or in an automated way.

A Production-Ready Service Is Stable and Reliable

- It has a standardized development cycle.
- Its code is thoroughly tested through lint, unit, integration, and end-to-end testing.
- Its test, packaging, build, and release process is completely automated.
- It has a standardized deployment pipeline, containing staging, canary, and production phases.
- Its clients are known.
- Its dependencies are known, and there are backups, alternatives, fallbacks, and caching in place in case of failures.
- It has stable and reliable routing and discovery in place.

A Production-Ready Service Is Scalable and Performant

- Its qualitative and quantitative growth scales are known.
- It uses hardware resources efficiently.
- Its resource bottlenecks and requirements have been identified.
- Capacity planning is automated and performed on a scheduled basis.
- Its dependencies will scale with it.

- It will scale with its clients.

- Its traffic patterns are understood.

- Traffic can be re-routed in case of failures.

- It is written in a programming language that allows it to be scalable and performant.

- It handles and processes tasks in a performant manner.

- It handles and stores data in a scalable and performant way.

A Production-Ready Service Is Fault Tolerant and Prepared for Any Catastrophe

- It has no single point of failure.

- All failure scenarios and possible catastrophes have been identified.

- It is tested for resiliency through code testing, load testing, and chaos testing.

- Failure detection and remediation has been automated.

- There are standardized incident and outage procedures in place within the microservice development team and across the organization.

A Production-Ready Service Is Properly Monitored

- Its key metrics are identified and monitored at the host, infrastructure, and microservice levels.

- It has appropriate logging that accurately reflects the past states of the microservice.

- Its dashboards are easy to interpret and contain all key metrics.

- Its alerts are actionable and are defined by signal-providing thresholds.

- There is a dedicated on-call rotation responsible for monitoring and responding to any incidents and outages.

- There is a clear, well-defined, and standardized on-call procedure in place for handling incidents and outages.

A Production-Ready Service Is Documented and Understood

- It has comprehensive documentation.

- Its documentation is updated regularly.

- Its documentation contains a description of the microservice; an architecture diagram; contact and on-call information; links to important information; an onboarding and development guide; information about the service's request flow(s), endpoints, and dependencies; an on-call runbook; and answers to frequently asked questions.

- It is well understood at the developer, team, and organizational levels.

- It is held to a set of production-readiness standards and meets the associated requirements.

- Its architecture is reviewed and audited frequently.

Evaluate Your Microservice

To help the reader evaluate the production-readiness of their microservice(s) and microservice ecosystem, Chapters 3–7 conclude with a short list of questions associated with the production-readiness standard discussed. The questions are organized by topic, and correspond to the sections within each chapter. All of the questions from each chapter have been collected here for easy reference.

Stability and Reliability

The Development Cycle

- Does the microservice have a central repository where all code is stored?
- Do developers work in a development environment that accurately reflects the state of production (e.g., that accurately reflects the real world)?
- Are there appropriate lint, unit, integration, and end-to-end tests in place for the microservice?
- Are there code review procedures and policies in place?
- Is the test, packaging, build, and release process automated?

The Deployment Pipeline

- Does the microservice ecosystem have a standardized deployment pipeline?
- Is there a staging phase in the deployment pipeline that is either full or partial staging?
- What access does the staging environment have to production services?

- Is there a canary phase in the deployment pipeline?
- Do deployments run in the canary phase for a period of time that is long enough to catch any failures?
- Does the canary phase accurately host a random sample of production traffic?
- Are the microservice's ports the same for canary and production?
- Are deployments to production done all at the same time, or incrementally rolled out?
- Is there a procedure in place for skipping the staging and canary phases in case of an emergency?

Dependencies

- What are this microservice's dependencies?
- What are its clients?
- How does this microservice mitigate dependency failures?
- Are there backups, alternatives, fallbacks, or defensive caching for each dependency?

Routing and Discovery

- Are health checks to the microservice reliable?
- Do health checks accurately reflect the health of the microservice?
- Are health checks run on a separate channel within the communication layer?
- Are there circuit breakers in place to prevent unhealthy microservices from making requests?
- Are there circuit breakers in place to prevent production traffic from being sent to unhealthy hosts and microservices?

Deprecation and Decommissioning

- Are there procedures in place for decommissioning a microservice?
- Are there procedures in place for deprecating a microservice's API endpoints?

Scalability and Performance

Knowing the Growth Scale

- What is this microservice's qualitative growth scale?
- What is this microservice's quantitative growth scale?

Efficient Use of Resources

- Is the microservice running on dedicated or shared hardware?
- Are any resource abstraction and allocation technologies being used?

Resource Awareness

- What are the microservice's resource requirements (CPU, RAM, etc.)?
- How much traffic can one instance of the microservice handle?
- How much CPU does one instance of the microservice require?
- How much memory does one instance of the microservice require?
- Are there any other resource requirements that are specific to this microservice?
- What are the resource bottlenecks of this microservice?
- Does this microservice need to be scaled vertically, horizontally, or both?

Capacity Planning

- Is capacity planning performed on a scheduled basis?
- What is the lead time for new hardware?
- How often are hardware requests made?
- Are any microservices given priority when hardware requests are made?
- Is capacity planning automated or is it manual?

Dependency Scaling

- What are this microservice's dependencies?
- Are the dependencies scalable and performant?
- Will the dependencies scale with this microservice's expected growth?

- Are dependency owners prepared for this microservice's expected growth?

Traffic Management

- Are the microservice's traffic patterns well understood?
- Are changes to the service scheduled around traffic patterns?
- Are drastic changes in traffic patterns (especially bursts of traffic) handled carefully and appropriately?
- Can traffic be automatically routed to other datacenters in case of failure?

Task Handling and Processing

- Is the microservice written in a programming language that will allow the service to be scalable and performant?
- Are there any scalability or performance limitations in the way the microservice handles requests?
- Are there any scalability or performance limitations in the way the microservice processes tasks?
- Do developers on the microservice team understand how their service processes tasks, how efficiently it processes those tasks, and how the service will perform as the number of tasks and requests increases?

Scalable Data Storage

- Does this microservice handle data in a scalable and performant way?
- What type of data does this microservice need to store?
- What is the schema needed for its data?
- How many transactions are needed and/or made per second?
- Does this microservice need higher read or write performance?
- Is it read-heavy, write-heavy, or both?
- Is this service's database scaled horizontally or vertically? Is it replicated or partitioned?
- Is this microservice using a dedicated or shared database?
- How does the service handle and/or store test data?

Fault Tolerance and Catastrophe-Preparedness

Avoiding Single Points of Failure

- Does the microservice have a single point of failure?
- Does it have more than one point of failure?
- Can any points of failure be architected away, or do they need to be mitigated?

Catastrophes and Failure Scenarios

- Have all of the microservice's failure scenarios and possible catastrophes been identified?
- What are common failures across the microservice ecosystem?
- What are the hardware-layer failure scenarios that can affect this microservice?
- What communication-layer and application-layer failures can affect this microservice?
- What sorts of dependency failures can affect this microservice?
- What are the internal failures that could bring down this microservice?

Resiliency Testing

- Does this microservice have appropriate lint, unit, integration, and end-to-end tests?
- Does this microservice undergo regular, scheduled load testing?
- Are all possible failure scenarios implemented and tested using chaos testing?

Failure Detection and Remediation

- Are there standardized processes across the engineering organization(s) for handling incidents and outages?
- How do failures and outages of this microservice impact the business?
- Are there clearly defined levels of failure?
- Are there clearly defined mitigation strategies?
- Does the team follow the five stages of incident response when incidents and outages occur?

Monitoring

Key Metrics

- What are this microservice's key metrics?
- What are the host and infrastructure metrics?
- What are the microservice-level metrics?
- Are all the microservice's key metrics monitored?

Logging

- What information does this microservice need to log?
- Does this microservice log all important requests?
- Does the logging accurately reflect the state of the microservice at any given time?
- Is this logging solution cost-effective and scalable?

Dashboards

- Does this microservice have a dashboard?
- Is the dashboard easy to interpret? Are all key metrics displayed on the dashboard?
- Can I determine whether or not this microservice is working correctly by looking at the dashboard?

Alerting

- Is there an alert for every key metric?
- Are all alerts defined by good, signal-providing thresholds?
- Are alert thresholds set appropriately so that alerts will fire before an outage occurs?
- Are all alerts actionable?
- Are there step-by-step triage, mitigation, and resolution instructions for each alert in the on-call runbook?

On-Call Rotations

- Is there a dedicated on-call rotation responsible for monitoring this microservice?
- Is there a minimum of two developers on each on-call shift?
- Are there standardized on-call procedures across the engineering organization?

Documentation and Understanding

Microservice Documentation

- Is the documentation for all microservices stored in a centralized, shared, and easily accessible place?
- Is the documentation easily searchable?
- Are significant changes to the microservice accompanied by updates to the microservice's documentation?
- Does the microservice's documentation contain a description of the microservice?
- Does the microservice's documentation contain an architecture diagram?
- Does the microservice's documentation contain contact and on-call information?
- Does the microservice's documentation contain links to important information?
- Does the microservice's documentation contain an onboarding and development guide?
- Does the microservice's documentation contain information about the microservice's request flow, endpoints, and dependencies?
- Does the microservice's documentation contain an on-call runbook?
- Does the microservice's documentation contain an FAQ section?

Microservice Understanding

- Can every developer on the team answer questions about the production-readiness of the microservice?
- Is there a set of principles and standards that all microservices are held to?
- Is there an RFC process in place for every new microservice?
- Are existing microservices reviewed and audited frequently?

- Are architecture reviews held for every microservice team?
- Is there a production-readiness audit process in place?
- Are production-readiness roadmaps used to bring the microservice to a production-ready state?
- Do the production-readiness standards drive the organization's OKRs?
- Is the production-readiness process automated?

Glossary

actionable alert

An alert that, when triggered, contains a step-by-step process that the **on-call rotation** can follow to triage, mitigate, and resolve the alert.

alerting

The practice of notifying an on-call developer (or developers) when one of a service's **key metrics** has reached a critical or warning **alert threshold**.

alert threshold

Static or dynamic quantities that are set for each **key metric** signifying that the key metric in question is at a normal, warning, or critical level; reaching the threshold should trigger an **actionable alert**.

application platform layer

The third layer of a microservice ecosystem, containing self-service internal tools, the development environment, test, package, build, and release tools, the deployment pipeline, microservice-level logging, and microservice-level monitoring.

application programming interface (API)

A well-defined client-side interface in each microservice that allows other services to interact with it programmatically by sending requests to static **endpoints**.

architecture diagram

A high-level visual representation of the architecture of a microservice.

architecture review

An organizational practice and process for evaluating, understanding, and improving the architecture of a microservice.

bare metal

The term used to refer to servers owned, run, and maintained by the organization itself, as opposed to hardware rented from so-called cloud providers.

canary

The second stage of the **deployment pipeline** containing a small percentage of servers hosting production traffic (2%–5% of production traffic); used to test new builds that have made it through **staging** before being rolled out to all **production** servers.

candidate for production

A build that has successfully passed all lint, unit, integration, and end-to-end tests in the **development cycle** and is ready to be introduced into the **deployment pipeline**.

capacity planning

The organizational practice of planned and scheduled **resource allocation**.

cloud providers

Companies such as Amazon Web Services (AWS), Google Cloud Platform (GCP), and Microsoft Azure that allow hardware resources to be rented and easily accessible over secure networks.

code testing

Tests that check syntax, style, individual components of a microservice, how the components work together, and how the microservice performs within its complex dependency chains; comprised of **lint tests**, **unit tests**, **integration tests**, and **end-to-end tests**.

communication layer

The second layer of the microservice ecosystem; contains the network, DNS, RPC frameworks, endpoints, messaging, service discovery, service registry, and load balancing.

concurrency

Applications and microservices that have concurrency break up each task into small pieces, rather than having just one process that does all of the work; essential property required for scalability.

continuous integration

A process that automatically integrates, tests, packages, and builds new changes to code on a scheduled and continuous basis.

Conway's Law

An informal "law" of software architecture named after Melvin Conway stating that the architectural structure of a company's products is determined by the communication patterns of the organization; see also **Inverse Conway's Law**.

dashboard

A visual, graphical display on an internal website containing graphs and charts of the health, status, behavior, and **key metrics** of an application, microservice, or system.

decommissioning

The process of retiring a microservice and/or its API endpoints so that they will no longer be available for use by upstream (client) services.

dedicated hardware

Servers or databases that host or store data for only one application, microservice, or system.

defensive caching

The practice of caching the data from a microservice's downstream dependencies to protect that microservice from suffering stability and reliability issues if the downstream dependency is unavailable.

dependency

A name for any other microservice that a microservice makes requests to; also refers to libraries that a microservice depends on; also used to refer to external (third-party) services that a microservice depends on.

deployment

The process through which a new build is sent to servers and the service is started.

deployment pipeline

The process of deploying new builds in three stages (to **staging**, to **canary**, and then to **production**).

deprecation

When a microservice and/or its endpoints are no longer being maintained by a development team and no longer recommended for use to upstream (client) services.

developer velocity

The speed at which development teams are able to iterate, roll out new features, and deploy.

development cycle

A name for the overall process associated with developing an application, microservice, or system.

development environment

A system containing tools, environment variables, and processes used by developers to write code for microservices.

endpoint

In this book, this term refers to the static API endpoints (HTTP, Thrift, etc.) of microservices that requests are routed to.

end-to-end tests

Tests that check whether changes to an application, service, or system work as expected by testing endpoints, clients, dependencies, and any databases.

external failures

Failures within the lower three layers of the microservice ecosystem stack.

full staging

When the **staging** phase of the **deployment pipeline** runs as a complete mirror copy of production.

growth scale

A name given to the measure of how an application, microservice, or system scales; every application, microservice, and system has two types of growth scales, a **quantitative growth scale** and a **qualitative growth scale**.

hardware layer

The first layer of the microservice ecosystem; contains physical servers, operating systems, resource isolation and abstraction, configuration management, host-level monitoring, and host-level logging.

hardware resources

See **resources**.

horizontal scaling

When an application or system is scaled by adding more servers (or other hardware resources).

host and infrastructure metrics

Key metrics of the lower three layers (**hardware layer**, **communication layer**, and **application platform layer**) of the **microservice ecosystem**.

host parity

When two separate environments, systems, or phases of the deployment pipeline (e.g., **staging** versus **production**) have the same number of hosts in each environment, system, datacenter, or deployment phase.

infrastructure

A term used in this book to refer to either the combination of the **application platform layer** and the **communication layer** or the three lowest layers of the microservice ecosystem (**hardware layer, communication layer**, and **application platform layer**.

integration tests

These test how the components of the microservice (which are tested individually using **unit tests**) work together.

internal failures

Failures within a microservice.

Inverse Conway's Law

The inverse of **Conway's Law**, which states that the organizational structure of a company is determined by the architecture of its product(s).

key metrics

Properties of an application, microservice, or system that are necessary and sufficient for describing the health, status, and behavior of the application, microservice, or system.

lint tests

Tests that check syntax and style errors; part of a **code-testing** suite.

load balancing

A device or service that distributes traffic across multiple servers or microservices.

logging

The practice of recording the events of an application, microservice, or system.

microservice

A small, replaceable, modular, independently developed and independently deployed software application that is responsible for performing one function within a larger system.

microservice ecosystem

A term for the overall system containing the microservices and infrastructure, which can be divided into four layers containing the microservices, the application platform, the communication layer, and the hardware layer.

microservice layer

The fourth layer of the microservice ecosystem; contains the microservices and all microservice-specific configurations.

microservice metrics

The **key metrics** unique to each **microservice** in the **microservice layer** of the **microservice ecosystem**.

monitoring

The practice of watching and tracking the status, health, and behavior of an application or microservice's **key metrics** over a long period of time.

monolith

Large, complex software systems that are maintained, run, and deployed as one single application containing all application-related code and features.

on-call rotation

A group of developers or operations engineers that are responsible for responding to, mitigating, and resolving an application, microservice, or system's alerts, incidents, and failures.

on-call runbook

A section of microservice documentation that contains general incident and outage response procedures, step-by-step instructions on how to triage, mitigate, and resolve each alert, and general tips on how to debug and troubleshoot the microservice; used by the developers or operational engineers who are on call for the service.

operational engineers

Engineers whose primary responsibilities are for the operational tasks associated with running a software application, including system administrators, TechOps, DevOps, and site reliability engineers.

outage

A period of time during which an application, microservice, or other system is inaccessible (experiencing downtime).

partial staging

When the **staging** phase of the **deployment pipeline** is not a complete mirror copy of production, but where microservices in the **staging** environment talk to the **production** versions of clients, dependencies, and databases.

partitioning

The process and architectural practice of breaking each task up into smaller pieces that can be processed in parallel; essential property of scalability.

production

The final stage of the **deployment pipeline** where all real-world traffic is hosted; also used to refer to real-world traffic and the environment hosting that traffic.

production-readiness audit

The process of evaluating a microservice's production-readiness using a **production-readiness checklist**.

production-readiness automation

A method for ensuring that microservices meet the production-readiness standards by automatically and programmatically checking whether each microservice adheres to the requirements associated with each production-readiness standard.

production-readiness checklist

A list of production-readiness standards, along with specific requirements that can be implemented to achieve each production-readiness standard.

production-readiness roadmap

A document used as part of the production-readiness process that details the steps that need to be taken to bring a microservice to a production-ready state.

production-readiness score

A score assigned to microservices that is calculated based on how well the microservice in question meets the requirements associated with each production-readiness standard.

publish–subscribe messaging

An asynchronous messaging paradigm in which clients subscribe to a topic, and will receive a message whenever a publisher publishes a message to that topic.

qualitative growth scale

A high-level, qualitative measure of how an application, microservice, or system scales that is tied to high-level business metrics; one type of **growth scale**.

quantitative growth scale

A quantitative measure of how an application, microservice, or system scales; obtained by translating the **qualitative growth scale** into a measurable quantity; one type of **growth scale**; usually expressed in terms of requests per second, queries per second, or transactions per second that the application, microservice, or system can process.

remote procedure call (RPC)

A call made over the network to a remote server that is designed to look and behave exactly like a local procedure call; used extensively in microservice architecture and in all large-scale distributed systems.

repository

A centralized archive where all the source code for an application or service is stored.

request flow

A name for the pattern of steps that are taken when a request is made from one microservice to another.

request–response messaging

A messaging paradigm in which a client will send a request to a **microservice** (or message broker) which will respond with the information requested.

resource allocation

Dividing available **hardware resources** across microservice ecosystems.

resource bottlenecks

Scalability limitations caused by the way an application, microservice, or system uses its **resources**.

resource requirements

The **resources** required by an application, microservice, or system.

resources

An abstraction of various performance properties of hardware (servers), like CPU, memory, network, etc.

self-service internal tools

Standardized tools in the **application platform layer** of a **microservice ecosystem** that are built to help developers work with the lower layers of the microservice ecosystem to develop, deploy, and run their microservices.

service discovery

A system that discovers where all instances of a microservice are hosted, ensuring that traffic is routed to the appropriate servers hosting the application.

service registry

A database that tracks all ports and IPs all of microservices and systems within a **microservice ecosystem**.

shared hardware

Servers or databases that are used to host or store data for more than one application, microservice, or system simultaneously.

single point of failure (SPOF)

A piece of an application, microservice, or system that, if it fails, will bring down the application, microservice, or system.

site reliability engineering (SRE)
Operational engineers responsible in large companies for the reliability of the applications, microservices, or systems within the engineering organization(s).

splitting the monolith
The name given to the process of breaking a large monolithic application into a set of microservices.

staging
The first phase of a **deployment pipeline** that does not serve production traffic and is used to test new builds; usually a mirror copy of **production**; may be implemented as either **full staging** or **partial staging**.

three-tier architecture
A basic architecture for software applications consisting of a frontend (client-side) piece, a backend piece, and some type of datastore.

unit tests
Small, independent tests that run over small pieces (or units) or a microservice's code; part of **code testing**.

vertical scaling
When an application or system is scaled by increasing the resources (CPU, RAM) of each host that the application or system is running on.

Index

A

alerts, 35, 106, 112-114, 140
Apache Kafka, 15
Apache Mesos, 63, 65
Apache Thrift endpoints, 10, 14
API (application programming interface) end-
    points, 9-11
    messaging to, 14
application architectures, 2-9
application platform, 16-19, 84, 86
application scalability, 3-5
architecture diagrams, 121
architecture reviews, viii, 126-127
audits, production-readiness, 127
automation, production-readiness, 128-129
availability, 26-28
Azure, 12

B

bad deployments, 82
bare metal, 12
bottlenecks, resource, 64, 65
bottlenecks, scalability, 65
Brooks, Frederick, 20, 38

C

caching, defensive, 54
canary environment, 50-51
candidates for production, 46
capacity planning, 65-67, 137
catastrophe-preparedness, 32-33
    (see also fault tolerance)
Celery, 15, 79
CentOS, 13

chaos testing, 32, 78, 90, 94-96
checklists
    for evaluation, 135-142
    for production-readiness, 131-133
circuit breakers, 55
cloud providers, 12
code comments, 119
code reviews, 44, 82
code testing, 32, 78, 90-91
communication, 14-16
    RPCs, endpoints, and messaging, 14
    service discovery, service registry, and load
        balancing, 15-16
communication paradigms, 14
communication-level failures, 84-86
company reorganization for microservice adop-
    tion, 8
competition for resources, 24
concurrency, 5
configuration management, 18
configuration management tools, 13
containerization, 63
Conway's Law, 21
    (see also Inverse Conway's Law)
coordination of incident response, 100
CPU requirements, 64

D

dashboards, 34, 51, 105, 110-112, 140
data storage, 10
    challenges of, 73
    choices in, 72-73
    scalability of, 31, 71-73, 138
database connection limitations, 73

Debian, 13
debugging logs, 110
decommissioning, 56, 136
dependencies, 53-55, 136
    documentation, 123
    failures, 86-88
    scaling, 31, 67-68, 137
dependency chains, 77
deployment failures, 82
deployment pipeline, 19, 44-53, 135
    canary environment, 50-51
    enforcing stable and reliable deployment,
        52-53
    load testing in, 93
    production, 51
    staging environment, 45-50
deprecation and decommissioning, 56, 136
design reviews, 82
development cycle, 18, 42-44, 135
development environments, 18
Docker, 65
documentation, 35-37, 117-130, 133, 141
    architecture diagram, 121
    contact and on-call information, 122
    description of service, 120
    FAQ section, 124
    links to repository, 122
    on-call runbooks section, 123-124
    onboarding and development section, 122
    overview, 117-119
    request flow, endpoint, and dependencies
        information, 123
    updating, 119
dynamic scaling, 15

E

Elastic Compute Cloud (AWS EC2), 12
Elastic Load Balancer (AWS ELB), 16
end-to-end tests, 91
endpoint documentation, 123
Eureka, 16
evaluation checklists, 135-142
external failures, 32

F

failures (see fault tolerance)
FAQ documentation, 124
fault tolerance, 32-33, 132, 139
    application platform-layer failures, 84-86

categorization of failures, 98-99
common cross-ecosystem failures, 81-83
communication-level failures, 84-86
dependency failures, 86-88
failure detection and mitigation, 23, 78, 80,
    96-97, 139
hardware failures, 83-84
identifying failure scenarios, 78, 139
incidents and outages, 97-102
internal (microservice) failures, 88
overview of potential failures and catastro-
    phes, 80-83
principles of, 77-79
resiliency testing, 89-96
review questions, 102
single points of failure, 78-80
follow-up, in incident response, 101
full staging, 46-47, 49

G
GitHub, 18
Google Cloud Platform (GCP), 12
growth scale, 31, 60-62, 66, 68, 137

H
HAProxy, 16
hardware, 12-13
hardware failures, 83-84
hardware requests planning, 66
hardware resource utilization, 63
health checks, 55
horizontal scaling, 4
host parity, 45
host-level logging, 13
host-level metrics, 106-108
host-level monitoring, 13
hotfixes, 53
HTTP+REST/THRIFT, 14
Hypertext Transfer Protocol (HTTP), 14

I
implementing production-readiness, 37-39
incident response, 97-102
    categorizing incidents and outages, 98-99
    five stages of, 99-102
    procedures for, 32
infrastructure development, 11-19
    (see also microservice ecosystem)

application platform, 16-19
communication, 14-16
hardware, 12-13
infrastructure metrics, 106-108
infrastructure requirements, 8
integration tests, 90
internal failures, 32, 88
Inverse Conway's Law, 21-22, 72

J

JSON data, 14

K

key functions identification, 7
key metrics, 68, 106-108, 110-112, 140
key metrics displays, 34
   (see also dashboards)
key metrics thresholds, 113

L

links documentation, 122
lint tests, 90
Linux, 13
load balancing, 3, 16
load testing, 32, 61, 69, 78, 90, 91-94
logging, 34, 51, 105, 109-110, 140
LRU (Least Recently Used) cache, 54

M

message broker, 14
messaging technologies, 14
metrics (see key metrics)
microservice (internal) failures, 88
microservice adoption from monolith, 7-9
microservice architecture, 9-11
   API endpoints, 9-11
   benefits of, 7
   challenges of, 1
   concept and goals of, 5-7
   data storage, 10
   remote procedure calls (RPCs), 10
   trade-offs of (see organizational challenges)
microservice ecosystem, 11-20
   application platform layer, 16-19, 84-86
   common failures across, 81-83
   communication layer, 14-16, 84-86
   creation of, 8
   hardware layer, 12-13, 83-84

microservice layer, 19-20, 86-88
microservice metrics, 106-108
microservice versioning, 109
microservice-level logging, 19
microservices
   categorizing, 98
   standards creation for, vii-ix
   umbrella principles for, vii
   understanding of (see understanding of
      microservices)
Microsoft Azure, 12
migration options, 8
mitigation, 101
monitoring, 34-35, 51, 68, 105-116, 132,
   140-141
   alerts, 112-114
   dashboards, 110-112
   key metrics, 106-108
   logging, 109-110
   on-call rotations, 114-115
   overview, 105-106
monolithic applications
   challenges of, 1
   scalability issues with, 4
   splitting into microservices, 7-9
monoliths, defined, 4
multiple-location datacenter issues, 69
The Mythical Man-Month (Brooks), 20, 38

N

Netflix Eureka, 16
Nginx, 16
NoSQL databases, 72

O

on-call information, 122
on-call rotations, 106, 114-115, 141
on-call runbooks, 113, 123-124
onboarding and development information, 122
operating systems, 13
operational failures, 81
organizational challenges, 20-24
   competition for resources, 24
   Inverse Conway's Law, 21-22
   mitigating failure, 23
   technical sprawl, 22-23
organizational understanding (see understanding of microservices)
outages, 97-102

P

partial staging, 48-50
partitioning, 5
performance, 33, 59
    (see also scalability and performance)
Phabricator, 18
postmortems, 101
predicting failures, 32-33
production, 51
production-readiness
    audits and roadmaps to, viii, 127, 128
    automation, 128-129
    checklist for, 131-133
    defining, viii
    standardization for (see standardization)
    standards implementation, 37-39
programming language limitations, 69-70
provisioning, 13
publish–subscribe (pubsub) messaging, 14

Q

qualitative growth scale, 61-62, 66, 67, 68
quantitative growth scale, 62, 66, 68
queries per second (QPS), 61

R

RabbitMQ, 15
RAM requirements, 64
README files, 119
Redis, 15, 79
relational databases, 72
reliability, 29-30, 41
    (see also stability and reliability)
remote procedure calls (RPCs), 10, 14
representational state transfer (REST) end-
    points, 14
request flow documentation, 123
request for comments (RFC), 126
requests per second (RPS), 61
request–response messaging, 14
resiliency testing, 32, 78, 89-96, 139
resolution of incidents, 101
resource allocation and distribution, 63
resource awareness, 64-65, 137
resource bottlenecks, 64, 65
resource isolation, 13
resource management, 13
resource requirements, 64

resource utilization, 33, 137
resources, competition for, 24
REST endpoints, 10
rollbacks, automated, 51
routing and discovery, 55, 136
runbooks, 113

S

scalability, 30-32
    (see also scalability and performance)
    in traffic handling, 31
    of applications, 3-5
    of data storage, 31
    of dependencies, 31
    of messaging, 15
    testing for (see load testing)
scalability and performance, 59, 131, 137-138
    bottlenecks, 65
    capacity planning, 65-67
    data storage, 71-73
    dependency scaling, 67-68
    efficient use of resources, 63
    principles of, 59-60
    resource awareness, 64-65
    task handling and processing, 69-71
    traffic management, 68-69
scaling
    dynamic, 15
    horizontal versus vertical, 65
self-service internal development tools, 17-18
service discovery, 15
service registry, 15
service-level agreements (SLAs), 26, 87, 97
Simian Army, 95
single points of failure, 78-80, 139
site reliability engineers (SREs), vii, 38
stability and reliability, 41, 131, 135-136
    dependencies, 53-55
    deployment pipeline, 44-53
    deprecation and decommissioning, 56
    development cycle, 42-44
    enforcement of, in deployment, 52-53
    importance of, 41-42
    principles of, 41-42
    routing and discovery, 55
    stability standards, 29-29
staging environment, 45-50
    candidates for production, 46
    full staging, 46-47, 49

partial staging, 48-50
purpose of, 49
standardization, 28-37
    availability measurement, 26-28
    challenges of, 25-26
    documentation and understanding, 35-37
    fault tolerance and catastrophe-
        preparedness, 32-33
    importance and implementation of, 37-39
    monitoring, 34-35
    performance, 33
    reliability, 29-30
    scalability, 30-32
    stability, 29-29

T

task handling and processing, 69-71, 138
    efficiency in, 70-71
    programming language limitations, 69-70
team communication and collaboration, 68
team structures, 21
technical debt reduction, 35
technical sprawl, 22-23
test data handling, 73
test tenancy, 49, 73

testing (see resiliency testing, code testing, load
    testing, chaos testing)
three-tier architecture, 2
traffic cycles, 51
traffic handling, 31
traffic management, 68-69, 138

U

Ubuntu, 13
understanding of microservices, 35-37,
    125-129, 133, 141
    architecture reviews, 126-127
    overview, 117-119
    production-readiness audits, 127
    production-readiness automation, 128-129
    production-readiness roadmaps, 128
unit tests, 90
uptime, 26

V

version control systems, 18
versioning, 10, 109
vertical scaling, 4

About the Author

Susan Fowler is a site reliability engineer at Uber Technologies, where she splits her time between running a production-readiness initiative across all Uber microservices and embedding within business-critical teams to bring their services to a production-ready state. She worked on application platforms and infrastructure at several small startups before joining Uber, and before that, studied particle physics at Penn, where she searched for supersymmetry and designed hardware for the ATLAS and CMS detectors.

Colophon

The animals on the cover of *Production-Ready Microservices* are leafcutter bees (of the genus *Megachile*). There are over 1,500 species of this insect, which is widespread throughout the world. One species from Indonesia, *Megachile pluto*, is thought to be the largest bee in the world: individuals can be up to 0.9–1.5 inches long.

Leafcutter bees gain their name from the female's common activity of cutting neat semicircles from the edges of leaves. She then carries these disc-shaped leaf pieces to her nest, which can be built in various places such as ready-made hollows, burrows in the ground, or rotting wood that the bee can bore into. Nests are between 4–8 inches long, cylindrical, and lined with leaf pieces in an overlapping pattern. These insects do not live in colonies, though it's possible for individuals to nest near each other.

The females arrange their nests in separate cells (building from the inside out) and lay one egg within each, along with a regurgitated pollen-and-nectar ball for the larva to eat. It is theorized that the leaves keep the larva's food from drying out until it can be eaten.

Adult bees also feed on nectar and pollen, and are very efficient pollinators due to their vigorous swimming-like motion while inside flowers (which shakes a great deal of pollen loose and coats the long hairs on the insect's abdomen). Females often need to take 10–15 trips to provision an individual nest cell, further increasing their effectiveness in cross-pollination. Thus, these bees are welcome inhabitants in many gardens and farms; artificial nesting boxes or tubes can be placed to attract them.

Many of the animals on O'Reilly covers are endangered; all of them are important to the world. To learn more about how you can help, go to *animals.oreilly.com*.

The cover image is from Lydekker's *Royal Natural History*. The cover fonts are URW Typewriter and Guardian Sans. The text font is Adobe Minion Pro; the heading font is Adobe Myriad Condensed; and the code font is Dalton Maag's Ubuntu Mono.

Learn from experts.
Find the answers you need.

Sign up for a **10-day free trial** to get **unlimited access** to all of the content on Safari, including Learning Paths, interactive tutorials, and curated playlists that draw from thousands of ebooks and training videos on a wide range of topics, including data, design, DevOps, management, business—and much more.

Start your free trial at:

oreilly.com/safari

(No credit card required.)